The Successes and Failures
of Economic Transition

Also by Hubert Gabrisch

EU ENLARGEMENT AND ITS MACROECONOMIC EFFECTS IN
EASTERN EUROPE
(*with Rüdiger Pohl*)

Also by Jens Hölscher

THE GERMANY CURRENCY UNION OF 1990: A Critical
Assessment (*with Stephen F. Frowen*)

50 YEARS OF THE GERMAN MARK: Essays in Honour
of Stephen F. Frowen

GLOBALIZATION OF CAPITAL MARKETS AND
MONETARY POLICY (*with Horst Tomann*)

GERMANY'S ECONOMIC PERFORMANCE:
From Unification to Euroisation

Within **Studies in Economic Transition** *series*
General Editors: Jens Hölscher and Horst Tomann

EAST GERMANY'S ECONOMIC DEVELOPMENT:
DOMESTIC AND GLOBAL ASPECTS (*with Anja Hochberg*)

FINANCIAL TURBULENCE AND CAPITAL MARKETS IN
TRANSITION COUNTRIES

MONEY, DEVELOPMENT AND ECONOMIC
TRANSFORMATION (*with Horst Tomann*)

The Successes and Failures of Economic Transition

The European Experience

Hubert Gabrisch and Jens Hölscher

First published 2006 by
PALGRAVE MACMILLAN
Houndmills, Basingstoke, Hampshire RG21 6XS and
175 Fifth Avenue, New York, N.Y. 10010
Companies and representatives throughout the world.

PALGRAVE MACMILLAN is the global academic imprint of the Palgrave Macmillan division of St. Martin's Press, LLC and of Palgrave Macmillan Ltd. Macmillan® is a registered trademark in the United States, United Kingdom and other countries. Palgrave is a registered trademark in the European Union and other countries.

ISBN-13: 978–1–4039–3493–2
ISBN-10: 1–4039–3493–2

This book is printed on paper suitable for recycling and made from fully managed and sustained forest sources.

A catalogue record for this book is available from the British Library.

Library of Congress Cataloging-in-Publication Data
    The successes and failures of economic transition: the European experience / edited by Hubert Gabrisch and Jens Hölscher.
        p. cm.
    Includes bibliographical references and index.
    ISBN 1–4039–3493–2 (cloth)
        1. Europe, Eastern – Economic policy – 1989– 2. Free enterprise – Europe, Eastern. 3. Post-communism – Europe, Eastern. I. Gabrisch, Hubert. II. Hölscher, Jens.
    HC244.S775 2006
    330.947—dc22   2006043163

10 9 8 7 6 5 4 3 2 1
15 14 13 12 11 10 09 08 07 06

Printed and bound in Great Britain by
Antony Rowe Ltd, Chippenham and Eastbourne

Contents

v

List of Figures

List of Tables

List of Boxes

List of Abbreviations

ALMP	Active labour market policies
BT	Balance of trade
CEE	Central and East European
CEEC	Central and East European countries
CPE	Centrally planned economy
EA	European Agreements
EBO	Employee buy-outs
EBRD	European Bank for Reconstruction and Development
ECE	Economic Commission for Europe
EMU	Economic and Monetary Union
EPL	Employment protection law
ERM	Exchange Rate Mechanism
ESCB	European System of Central Banks
FCL	Foreign currency loan
FDI	Foreign direct investment
FEER	Fundamental equilibrium exchange rates
FRG	Federal German Republic (West Germany)
FSU	Former Soviet Union
FTA	Free trade area
FX/forex	Foreign exchange
GATT	General Agreement on Tariffs and Trade
GDP	Gross domestic product
GDR	German Democratic Republic (East Germany)
ILO	International Labour Organization
IMF	International Monetary Fund
JV	Joint venture
LIS	Luxembourg Income Study
LOLR	Lender of last resort
MBO	Management buy-outs
MEBO	Management–employee buy-outs
MoF	Ministry of Finance
MTBF	Medium-term budget framework
NAFTA	North American Free Trade Area
NAIRU	Non-accelerating inflation rate of unemployment
NCA	National competition authorities
NCF	Net capital flows

NGO	Non-governmental organization
NIC	Newly industrialized country
NIK	Supreme Chamber of Control (Poland)
OST	Optimal speed of transition
PC	Personal computer
PPP	Purchasing power parity
REER	Real exchange rate
SBC	'Soft' budget constraints
SEE	South East European
SGP	Stability and growth pact
SME	Small and medium-sized enterprise
SOE	State-owned enterprise
TI	Transparency International
TVE	Township and Village Enterprise (China)
UNCTAD	United Nations Conference on Trade and Development
VAT	Value added tax
WTO	Word Trade Organization

Acknowledgements

We thank Michael Kaser, who provided detailed suggestions and constructive comments on an earlier draft of the book. We gratefully acknowledge the assistance of Silva Globacnik and Pavel Silan in obtaining insights into restructuring and privatization of the Gorenje company. Further, we have to thank the organizers and students of the European University VIADRINA in Frankfurt/Oder, Germany (MBA – Management for Central and Eastern Europe), where we had the opportunity to teach parts of this book. Special thanks go to Peter Kunz and Hans-Jürgen Wagener.

Furthermore we like to thank Éva Katalin Polgár for preparing the case study of Hungary. Mariusz Jarmużek and Johannes Stephan have been collaborating with us in various projects on which this book is based so that is almost impossible to identify the impact they had on this book.

Parts of the article by Jens Hölscher, 'Income Distribution and Convergence in the Transition Process – A Cross Country Comparison', in *Comparative Economic Studies*, (2) (June 2006), Palgrave Macmillan, have been reproduced with permission of Palgrave Macmillan, and parts of the article by Jens Hölscher and Johannes Stephan, 'Competition Policy in Central East Europe in the Light of EU Accession', in *Journal of Common Market Studies*, 42(2) (2004), have been reproduced with the permission of Blackwell Publishing.

Finally, we wish to thank Keith Povey for meticulous editorial support.

HUBERT GABRISCH
JENS HÖLSCHER

Introduction

This book addresses the need for a better understanding of the processes of transformation from a socialist economic system towards a market economy. If we consider the 1917 Revolution in Russia as the ignition point of one of the greatest social experiments of mankind, the transformation processes since 1989 are the major challenges at the turn of the twenty-first century. The reader will find that the world was not very well prepared for these challenges. There was no 'master plan' in the drawer, despite the fact that 'system competition' between communism and capitalism had lasted for decades. On the eve of the collapse of the socialist economic system much hope for a better world under the triumphant market economy was generated. With the benefit of hindsight these hopes look naïve after fifteen years of ongoing transformation.

The book is divided into nine chapters. Chapter 1 introduces the reader to what is understood as 'transformation' and how it is actually measured. The word 'transformation' might refer to the development from a chrysalis into a butterfly, but this analogy does not hold for the complex change in economic systems. One obvious problem is the determination of the beginning and the end of systemic change. Chapter 1 discusses these aspects, and presents some stylized facts.

Chapter 2 presents two different intellectual concepts of transformation. The earlier concept was called the 'Washington Consensus' and dominated economic policy in transition countries for a long time. This approach was based on liberalization, privatization and stabilization as cornerstones of the transformation to a market economy. This approach is contrasted with the 'evolutionary–institutionalist' concept, which emphasizes the role of informal institutions such as behaviour and mindsets, as well as formal institutions such as the rule of law. This approach takes into account that institution building is a time-consuming process, in particular when some institutions within the transition countries, such as those of the financial sector, had to be built up from scratch. The chapter concludes with a taxonomy of different countries in transformation.

Chapter 3 analyses the emerging financial sector, the transition from a non-money to a money economy, in the context of stability and growth. It begins with the necessity to build the major institution of the modern market economy, the central bank: a sound financial sector should contribute to macroeconomic stability and economic growth. A strategy of semi-liberalization is discussed against the background of financial fragility in order to safeguard the evolution of financial institutions such as commercial banks and capital markets. Compared with the European Union, these institutions are still underdeveloped in post-socialist countries.

Chapter 4 reviews the process of privatization, the fostering of *de novo* firms, and the emergence of competition. Competition is the driving force of an innovative market economy with private ownership. But privatization – the core of ownership transformation – is a necessary policy to generate a competitive private sector, although it is far from being sufficient. We discuss the problem of the 'soft' budget constraint, which prevails in *centrally planned economies* (CPEs) with state-owned firms and which is a stubborn attendant of transition, when ownership transformation is conducted in a non-competitive way and in a non-competitive environment. A taxonomy of privatization presents the various ways in which ownership transformation was pursued. Finally the difficulties with creating a competitive environment are illustrated with an analysis of anti-trust policy in transformation countries.

Chapter 5 is an in-depth investigation of the emerging labour market and the unemployment problem. The latter is particularly crucial in transition countries as the socialist regime operated with full employment and the transformation introduced unemployment as a formerly unknown, or at least hidden, phenomenon. Generally transformation goes along with rising unemployment, which stabilises at certain levels and which differ in the various countries under observation. Aspects such as labour market rigidities and 'jobless growth' are discussed. Finally the unemployment–output relationship is analysed.

Chapter 6 puts the post-socialist countries into the global market place. External shocks from international trade and capital flows are discussed. The question of gradual or shock liberalization is discussed against a background of the vulnerability to speculative attacks. In this view a distinction between welcome and undesired capital inflows is made, and the exchange rate becomes a strategic variable.

Chapter 7 reviews rising income inequality during transformation. It is found that the 'standard explanation' does not apply to transition countries. A wealth of information about functional and personal income distribution is provided and it can be observed that the initially rising inequality stabilizes at continental European levels in Central and East Europe (CEE), but continues to rise in Russia. The question of whether the curve of this development can be describe as an inverted U-shape like the Kuznets curve is discussed against the background of convergence and divergence.

Chapter 8 takes a closer look at those post-socialist countries which became members of the European Union in 2004. Membership put those economies on the same level playing field as the mature market economies of the west European countries, which makes competition policy within the enlarged union a major challenge for successful transformation. In addition, EU membership means that the transition countries will have to adopt the Euro and join the European Monetary Union (EMU). To take this step they have to fulfil the stability criteria of the Maastricht treaty and fiscal discipline imposes a further challenge for these new EU members, as the necessary transparency of state income and expenditure cannot be assumed.

Finally, Chapter 9 concludes the book with a comparison of the various paths of transformation in different countries. These are presented as case studies. East Germany, Russia, Hungary, and China are selected, because these countries demonstrate different types of transformation.

1
The Meaning and Measurement of Transition

Chapter 1 introduces the reader to the characteristics of economic transition. We explain transition as a fundamental change in institutions, and show that progress in transition has been made above all in changing formal institutions; the transformation of informal institutions, however, still lags behind. Corruption, little interpersonal trust and trust in public institutions cause high forgone gains in income generation, employment, and equity. We further evaluate the achievements of institutional changes in terms of sustainable and equitable economic development, and compare expected with actual results. We find that differences between the Chinese transition and transition in Russia and other CEE countries can be explained by country-specific institutional arrangements.

What transition means

Transition from a socialist CPE to a market economy is a phenomenon that attracted the attention of economists and politicians all over the world in the early 1990s when the Soviet empire in Europe and Central Asia collapsed, and the Cold War bi-polar world dissolved at the same time. The dissolution of Yugoslavia, an independent associate of the socialist world with workers' self-government followed. Transition had actually started some years earlier, in 1978, with the path-breaking political changes and economic reforms in China. But in the Cold War world, communist China and Yugoslavia played a minor role in the thinking of politicians and economists compared with the Soviet Union and European socialist countries. With the decay of the Soviet empire, the interest of economists in transition issues rose. A host of books and articles have been written, many conferences have taken place, and new organizations have been established to study the problems of transition, or to assist the CEE countries in their transition. They view the general and specific transition issues from their own perspectives – macroeconomics, microeconomics, institutional economics, political economics, business economics, sociology, or political science. Not all such provide a clear-cut definition of what transition might be, but implicitly they would all accept that 'transition' in its broadest sense means a fundamental change in a society's economic, social, political and cultural *institutions*.

Institutions consist of *formal rules*, or laws, as well as *informal rules* – the norms, conventions and commonly shared values that are characteristic of the culture of a given society. Formal rules, for example, include the establishment of property rights, of competition, and of private ownership. They also include rules on regulation and protection where the important role of the government and the central bank comes into play. Transition from a socialist to a market economy is not only a change in the formal rules of how the society or economy has to work, but also of the informal rules. The set of institutions represents the society's *social capital* (Box 1.1).

Rules are created by explicit and implicit *social contracts*. Formal rules can be decreed by the government or by the courts, or they can be written down in contracts by interested parties. Behind each explicit contract stands an implicit contract based on norms and values. Informal rules cannot be decreed, but develop in a long-lasting trial-and-error process. The transition of a CPE into a market economy always implies a fundamental change in the formal role the state plays in the society and economy, but the expected results of this change can be achieved only when also the informal rules have adjusted to this change. Here, transition means the role of the state in the consciousness of the individuals, particularly the change of expectations formulated

---

Box 1.1 Social capital

In recent years this term was made popular by Robert D. Putnam (Putnam 2000). Institutions create the social capital of an economy. Whereas physical capital refers to physical objects and human capital refers to the properties of individuals, social capital refers to *connections among individuals* – social networks, and the norms of reciprocity and trustworthiness that arise from them. In that sense, social capital is closely related to what some have called 'civic virtue'. The difference is that 'social capital' calls attention to the fact that civic virtue is most powerful when embedded in a network of reciprocal social relations. A society of many virtuous but isolated individuals is not necessarily rich in social capital. Social capital plays a leading role in modern innovation theory, which assumes that knowledge is socially constructed. The term is used by many empirical studies trying to describe informal institutions.

over many years on the basis of the entitlements the individuals hold against the paternalistic state. One striking example is the risk-averse mentality that emerges in a socialist society.

Educated in such a mentality, individuals are confronted with the necessity to be more flexible or even to show an entrepreneurial capacity. A broad segment of the transforming society might passively react to the new challenges and wait for traditional government action. The other extreme is a kind of early capitalist behaviour, ruthlessly exploiting the ignorance of others or the lack of regulation that protects the poor.

Since norms, values, and conventions change only over time, they are a constraint on the effectiveness of the new formal rules for the interaction between state and individual. This creates a severe problem of predictability: the result of the change in formal rules might become unpredictable when norms and values do not adjust appropriately, and individuals try to shift the risk of their actions to the state. To provide two examples: a market economy is based on *financial contracts*, which are charged over time. A creditor can never be absolutely certain that a debtor will repay. Formal institutions such as law enforcement, property rights, and the availability of collateral help to establish a relation of mutual confidence between the debtor and the creditor. A culture of repaying debt bolsters these formal rules. These institutions were more or less unknown in the socialist economy – financial contracts did not play a meaningful role in the economy, nor did money in its basic functions. Debt was a non-financial, non-public favour one individual gave to another, and this debt was also paid back by a non-financial favour. Financial relations are something new and many people do not yet trust each other.

The second example concerns the issue of *prices* and their different roles in a CPE and a market economy. Prices are controlled by the state in a CPE, but are flexible in a market economy. State-controlled or flexible market prices – this is a matter of formal rules, which can be changed simply by governmental decree. However, in a market economy, prices reflect the expectations of agents about the scarcity of resources with respect to requirements in the future. Agents formulate their expectations under the given institutional environment. They trust the price system as guide for their decisions when the institutional environment is stable. A change of the formal rules confuses the system of expectations, and economically founded expectations cannot longer be formulated.

These examples lead to the general conclusion that institutions are relatively stable sets of widely shared and realized expectations about the behaviour of people. Expectations are deeply rooted in experiences from the past and are linked to the social capital. From a standpoint of general economic theory, institutions serve to internalize external economies.

The costs of institution building are called *transaction costs*. They include the costs agents have to bear for investigating the trustworthiness of their contract partners.

In general, the most important role of the state is to intervene in the economy when the transaction costs in relations between individual agents become too high, and cheating each other spreads. A typical example is *asymmetric information* on financial markets: a bank has better information about the return on financial investment than its clients. Working with the client's money, the bank can undertake more risky operations; this problem is called *moral hazard*. If the cost for verifying their bank's fealty is too high for the clients, financial fragility of the banking sector will increase and threaten the stability of the entire economy. Therefore, the government intervenes to regulate and supervise the financial sector. Another example is infrastructure, where the provider may have difficulty in charging everyone who takes advantage of it. If this is a general problem, the state provides infrastructural investment and raises taxes to finance it. Finally, economic stability reduces transaction costs, since it stabilizes private expectations and is therefore a core task for the state.

However, the role of the state during transition from a planned to a market economy is completely different to the standard case in economic theory. The transition of a CPE/society will necessarily lead to a general depreciation of all former information and increase the risks of economic agents being burdened with negative external economies, caused by the behaviour of other agents. What is more, while the state in general economic theory takes an external position when setting rules for the society, it is subject to fundamental changes during transition. Djankov *et al.* (2003) described this problem as the move from 'dictatorship to disorder'. A desertion by the state of its various tasks might cause severe losses in social welfare and economic growth; transaction costs might become too high due to the informational chaos and the lack of contract enforcement.

How transition is measured

Attempts to measure progress in transition in Eastern Europe and Central Asia (the successor states of the Soviet empire and of Yugoslavia) have been made by economists since the early 1990s. Apart from a scientific interest in this undertaking, these studies were motivated by a wish to evaluate the competence of transition countries to join the international communities, among them prominently the World Trade Organization (WTO) and the European Union. One of the EU criteria for accepting new members is that the candidate has achieved a 'functioning' market economy.

Although an interdisciplinary approach would be necessary to understand progress towards a functioning market economy, much of the literature initially concentrated on measuring formal institution building. The European Bank for Reconstruction and Development (EBRD) provides probably the best-known attempt to measure transition (see Table 1.1). The EBRD has calculated 'transition indicators' for twenty-six CEE countries, the Baltic states, and the Commonwealth of Independent States (CIS) since 1994. The indicators measure only the change in formal institutions; when the Bank uses the term 'institution' (as in the case of 'non-banking institutions'), it means 'organization' and legal regulation.[1] A comparison between the first *Transition Report* of 1994 and the *Transition Report* of 2003 illustrates what was on the agenda of transition in both an early and in a later stage. While the liberalization of prices and trade, privatization, enterprise reform, the foreign exchange system, and banking reform were top of the agenda in the first stage of transition, competition, infrastructure, interest rate liberalization, security markets and non-banking institutions, the infrastructure, and the legal environment were the key issues of the later stage of transition.

The EBRD indicators do not view a specific market economy. Progress in transition is measured against the standards of industrialised market economies, recognizing that there is neither a perfectly functioning market economy nor a unique end-point for transition. These indicators reflect a kind of minimum requirements, taking into account all 'real existing' market economies in industrialized countries (OECD

Table 1.1   EBRD transition indicators, 2003

Enterprises	Markets and Trade	Financial institutions	Infrastructure reform	Legal transition indicators
Privatization (small- and large-scale) Restructuring and governance	Price liberalization Trade and foreign exchange system Competition policy	Banking reform Interest rate liberalization Security markets and non-banking institutions	Utilities (water, railroads, energy)	Legal extensiveness, legal effectiveness

Source: EBRD (2003).

countries). Based on the EBRD approach, one can calculate a total index for the year. Figure 1.1 shows this index for 2003. The eight countries that joined the European Union in 2004 received the highest scores in formal transition progress with Hungary as the most advanced transition country (almost 90 per cent of a 'standard' market economy). Moldova, Russia, Albania, Ukraine, Belarus, and Bosnia and Herzegovina form the lower end of the progress continuum.

De Melo, Denizer and Gelb (1996) developed a composite transition index including China and Vietnam, unfortunately only for 1994. This composite indicator builds upon a wide range of policy reforms referred to as 'economic liberalization', reflected in an early EBRD indicator set. Comparing both sets for this single year, China and Vietnam already belonged to the advanced reformers, being in one group with almost all the later EU accession countries.

The recent economic literature has made some progress in measuring the effects of well-established as well as defective norms, values, and other informal institutions (Box 1.2). One of the best-known indicators for world-wide deficiencies in norms and behaviour is the Corruption Index developed and calculated by Transparency International, a non-governmental organization (NGO). The Corruption Index measures the

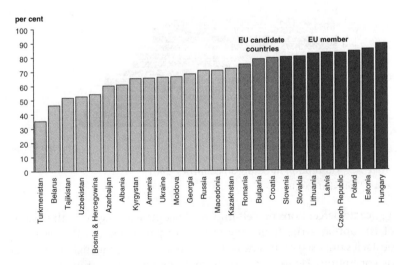

Figure 1.1   Progress[a] in transition, 2003

Note:
[a] Total scores for each country were calculated by adding the scores of 11 single EBRD indicators. The highest score for an indicator is 4+ (4.3), hence the highest score is 47.3 (11 × 4.3).

Sources: EBRD (2004); own calculations.

Box 1.2   Defective informal institutions: corruption and mistrust

Corruption is the misuse of public power for private benefit, and reflects the mistrust of private agents in law, enforcement, and markets, the loose binding of state officers to the rules of giving state orders. It also reflects below a mismatch between reforms of the state administration and the engagement of state officers according to education and qualification. Corruption yields economic losses: the transaction costs of a corrupt society are higher than those of a non-corrupt society, for a corrupt society is less transparent. The risk of excluding efficient solutions from being accepted by a state officer is higher in a less transparent public sphere.

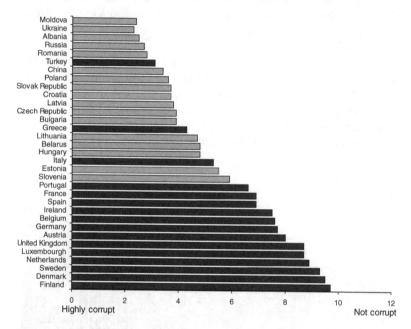

Figure 1.2   Corruption in European countries, 2001
Source: Lambsdorf (2003).

aggregate perceptions of well-informed people with regard to the extent of corruption – the frequency of corrupt payments and the resulting obstacles imposed on business. The lower the index, the higher the level of corruption: Figure 1.2 reveals that the level of corruption is still higher in transition countries than in EU countries.

The institution of trust reduces the cost of transactions – that is, of gaining reliable information about contract partners, or about the

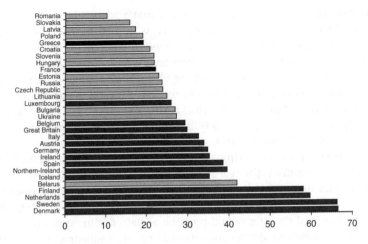

Figure 1.3 Interpersonal trust
Source: Halman (2001).

government and the central bank. A study by Zak *and* Knack (2001) found that high-trust societies produce more output than low-trust societies. The *European Values Studies* include four dimensions of social capital: interpersonal trust ('Can people be trusted?'), institutional trust ('How much confidence one has into public institutions – church, government, army ...'), participation in civil societies (parties, trade unions ...), and trustworthiness ('cheating on taxes ...') (Schaik 2002). The question asked reads: 'Generally speaking, would you say that most people can be trusted?' 'Figure 1.3 provides results of the 2000 *European Values Survey*, indicating that interpersonal trust is low in transition countries compared with EU countries. While more than 40 per cent (mean value) of the respondents in EU countries expressed trust in most people, the ratio was about 20 per cent in transition countries.

An alternative measure: economic and social effects

It is not just the creation of [a] market economy that matters, but the improvement of living standards and the establishment of the foundations of sustainable, equitable, and democratic development.
   Joseph E. Stiglitz (Nobel Prize Laureate in Economics, 2001)

The observation and measurement of institutional change is one concept that can demonstrate the movement from a centrally planned to a market economy. This simply assumes that a market economy, once established, provides the economic success desired by the nations in transition. However, this assumption is not *a priori* guaranteed, for we find market economies at a weak economic level nation-wide, or with a significant split in incomes and welfare among their population, and with authoritarian government, although market institutions ensure an efficient allocation of production factors at the micro level. The institutional concept of measurement needs to be completed by the measurement of the economic and social effects of transition at the macro level.

The basic figure measuring the improvement of living conditions of an entire economy is the real gross domestic product (GDP). The widespread idea that economists have of the relationship between transition and GDP is the J-curve (Figure 1.4a). It sounds plausible that the shocks of institutional changes would provoke a sharp decline in output, and that initial losses would be compensated only after adjustments of firms, private households, and the government. Finally, when transition was more or less completed, the post-socialist economy would enter a path of steady and high growth rates of output, ensuring a catching-up of *per capita* income with that of market economies. But the J-curve is theoretically ambiguous in the literature on transition. The underlying idea is based on the colourful expression 'creative destruction', introduced by the Austrian economist Joseph Schumpeter (1883–1950) in his famous 1942 book (Schumpeter 1975, pp. 82–85). The term describes Schumpeter's view of the process of industrial transition that follows radical innovation. The emergence of new entrepreneurs is seen as the force that sustains the long-term economic growth of a capitalist economy, even as it destroys the value of established companies that previously enjoyed some degree of monopoly power. Intuition would suggest that the creation of free markets for entrepreneurs in a former socialist economy is similar to the destruction of state-owned monopolies, and competition of many ideas would be the basis for innovation and knowledge generation. It is, however, not clear whether the J-curve idea includes a decline in *absolute* output or a decline of the *growth rate* of output; neither is it clear how strongly output will fall, and how long the transitional shocks will last. Some economists and politicians assume a 'very short' period (about six months) before the liberalized economy resumes growth.

Actually, the J-curve seems to be a stylized course of transition in the CEE countries (see Figure 1.4b). Here, the decline of GDP reached 30 per cent – almost 50 per cent (the former German Democratic Republic, GDR) compared with the last pre-transition year of 1989.

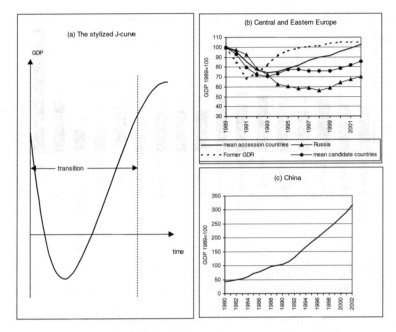

Figure 1.4 The J-curve and actual GDP development: unweighted means (accession countries: Czech Republic, Estonia, Hungary, Latvia, Lithuania, Poland, Slovakia, Slovenia; candidate countries: Bulgaria, Romania, Croatia)

Sources: UN–ECE (1998, 2003, 2004); International Monetary Fund (2003).

Output collapse was comparable to another unique event in world history, the Great Depression of 1928–1930. The course of output seems far from being a J-curve in Russia and in South-Eastern Europe, the case of China even demonstrates that transition does not necessarily entail a collapse of output at all. China has reported a steady growth of output since 1979.

Usually a nation's prosperity is not measured in terms of its total GDP. If the objective of growth is the material welfare of the nation's individuals, then the proper measure of the success of a program of economic transition is how much it adds to GDP per capita. Figure 1.5 shows how well and how differently the transition countries performed in aggregate economic terms. Among the eight EU accession countries of 2004, the Czech Republic, Estonia, Hungary, Poland, the Slovak Republic, and Slovenia achieved a higher GDP per capita in 2002, compared with 1989. Latvia and Lithuania were still below their point of departure, followed by Bulgaria, Romania, and Croatia, the future accession countries. The most impressive difference is between the European transition

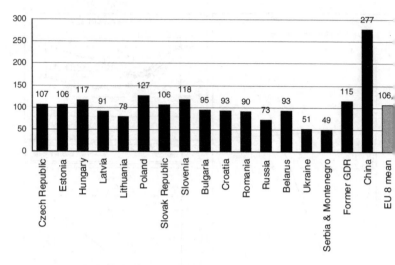

Figure 1.5   Real GDP *per capita*, 2002 (1989 = 100)

Sources: UN–ECE (1998, 2003, 2004); International Monetary Fund (2003).

countries and China. China achieved an increase in total output p◄ capita of about 277 per cent between 1989 and 2002, and more than 60 per cent between 1978 and 2002.

Equitable growth supports trust building and economic growth. Wit regard to income distribution, transition can end in more inequalit with private entrepreneurship, a functional income re-distribution fro◄ wage to profit income was to be expected. Equality of wages was a sig of the socialist economy. Inequality is, however, measured as person◄ income distribution, which is not only affected by functional distrib◄ tion, but also by tax and pension policies. Figure 1.6 shows the develo◄ ment of GDP per capita through the changes in the Gini coefficient (s◄ the Appendix, p. 17). The most dramatic increase in inequality ha◄ pened in China, however, GDP in both absolute and per capita terms ◄ least grew. In CEE transition countries, inequality was coupled with collapse in output.

At the beginning of transition, poverty was not what most economis and politicians expected. But output collapse and rising income inequa ity (see Chapter 7 for a more detailed analysis) is always a cause ◄ poverty. Poverty is more than hunger or a decline in consumption poss bilities. Increasing poverty is often accompanied by the spread of diseas◄ a decline in fertility, an increase in mortality, depopulation, criminaliz◄ tion, the growth in corruption, and reduced access to education.

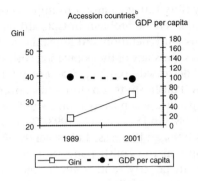

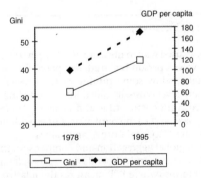

Figure 1.6 GDP per capita and the Gini coefficient[a]

Notes:

[a] Gini coefficients are based on the distribution of earnings interpolated from group data for monthly earnings, with bonuses, for full-time employees as reported by employers.

[b] Poland: 1999; Estonia: 2000.

Source: UN–ECE (2004).

Absolute poverty (Box 1.3) at a daily consumption of less than $2 per day *per capita* is not a serious problem in CEE, although it temporarily increased in the Russian Federation and Romania to 20 per cent of the population. In China, the share of the population with an daily consumption of less than $2 decreased from 70 per cent in 1990 to 47 per cent in 2000 in China. A Polish study on long-run poverty development documented a sharp increase of poverty from about 5 per cent of the population in the early 1980s to 15 per cent in 1993. The poverty rate declined between 1994 and 1998, and increased consistently after that date. The share of poor people in the Polish population was at 15.2 per cent, measured as 'moderate poverty', and at 9.6 per cent, measured as 'deep poverty' in 2001. Among the EU accession and candidate countries, only the Czech Republic and Slovenia had lower poverty rates (World Bank 2004).

Similar to income inequality, transition led to a redistribution of wealth. While in socialism the population hold assets mainly in form of money stocks, complemented with some non-money privileges of the communist party *nomenclatura*, the rising income inequality and the privatization process contributed to more inequality in money and real assets. In almost all countries the *nomenclatura* was able to acquire some of the ownership of state-owned enterprises in a non-regulated, illegal, way ('spontaneous privatization'), In Russia (and the Ukraine), in particular, a new class of rich emerged, the so-called oligarchs. An 'oligarch' is

---

Box 1.3   Absolute and relative poverty

The most commonly used way to measure *absolute poverty* is based on incomes or consumption levels. A person is considered 'poor' if his or her consumption or income level falls below some minimum level necessary to meet basic needs. This minimum level is usually called the 'poverty line'. What is necessary to satisfy basic needs varies across time and societies. Therefore, poverty lines vary in time and place, and each country uses lines which are appropriate to its level of development, societal norms, and values.

For the purpose of global aggregation and comparison, the World Bank uses reference lines set at $1, $2, and $4 per day and *per capita* in 1993 purchasing power parity (PPP) terms (where PPP measures the relative purchasing power of currencies across countries). This is an absolute poverty measure, applied to countries of different climatic zones (for example, with and without expenditure for heating). An alternative approach is *relative poverty*: this concept measures poverty as the share of persons in households which have an income or expenditure below half of the average for the country in which they live. This national poverty-line approach has been adopted by the European Union.

a member of a small group of powerful people who have a significant influence on the government of a country. Today, the term is commonly used to describe the political-economic outcomes of the ill-conducted Russian privatization process. This group consists of about 600 owners of privatized enterprises (Guriev and Rachinsky, 2005). In all countries, but particularly in Russia, oligarchs contributed to the spread of mistrust against private ownership, state administration and to the weakening of democratic development. Chapter 9 returns to the issue of oligarchs in the case of the Russian transition.

Appendix A: the Gini coefficient and the Lorenz curve

The Gini coefficient was developed by the Italian statistician Corrado Gini (1884–1965). What it means and how it can be calculated is shown in Figure 1A.1.

The horizontal axis plots the cumulative percentage of the population whose inequality is under consideration, starting from the poorest and ending with the richest. In the case presented, we have 10 household deciles. The vertical axis plots the cumulative percentage of income associated with the units on the horizontal axis. In the case of a completely egalitarian income distribution in which each household decile has the same share in total income, the Lorenz curve would be

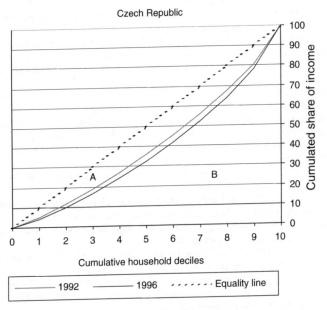

Figure 1A.1 Income distribution and the Gini coefficient

the dashed straight 45° line. When inequality exists, the poor population has proportionately lower share of income compared with the rich population, an the Lorenz curve take the form of curve below the 45° line. When inequality rise so the Lorenz curve moves towards the bottom right-hand corner. B is the enti area under or above the equal distribution line, and the area between the equ distribution and the Lorenz curve is A. The Gini coefficient may be given as a pr portion or percentage of A in B. The Gini coefficient will be equal to 0 when th distribution is completely egalitarian. If the society's total income accrues to on one person/household unit, leaving the rest with no income at all, then the Gir coefficient will be equal to 1, or 100 per cent. Figure 1A.1 presents the Czec Republic, and will be discussed and compared in greater detail in Chapter 7 (p. 12C

Note

1. In its more recent reports, the EBRD made attempts to include inform institutions in the assessment of legal transition indicators.

References and further reading

De Melo, Martha, Cevdet Denizer, and Alan Gelb (1996) 'From plan to marke patterns of transition', *World Bank Policy Research Working Paper*, No. 1564.

Djankov, Simeon, Edward Glaeser, Rafael La Porta, Florencio Lopez-de-Silane and Andrej Shleifer (2003) 'The new comparative economics', *Journal Comparative Economics*, 31, 595–619.

EBRD (European Bank for Reconstruction and Development), *Transition Repo* (London: EBRD, several years).

Guriev, Sergei, and Andrei Rachinsky (2005) 'The role of oligarchs in Russian cap italism', *Journal of Economic Perspectives*, 19, 131–51.

Halman, L. (2001) '*The European Values Study: A Third Wave*' (Tilburg: Tilbu University).

International Monetary Fund (2001 and 2003) *International Financial Statistic* (Washington, DC: IMF).

Lambsdorf, J. G. (2003) 'Corruption Perception Index 2003', Transparenc International, *Global Corruption Report 2003*, 262–266, available http://www.globalcorruptionreport.org/download/gcr2004/12_Corruptio research_I.pdf (5 July 2004).

Putnam, R. D. (2000) *The Collapse and Revival of American Community* (New Yor Simon & Schuster).

Schaik, T. van (2002) *Social Capital in the European Values Study Surveys*, paper pr pared for the OECD–ONS international conference on social capital measure ment, London, September; available at http://www.uvt.nl/faculteiten/few economie/schaik/evsoecd.pdf (6 July 2005).

Schumpeter, J. A. (1975) *Creative Destruction: Capitalism, Socialism and Democrac* (New York: Harper, orig. pub. 1942).

Stiglitz, J. (2000) 'Wither reform? Ten years of transition,' in B. Pleskovic an J.E. Stiglitz (eds), *Annual World Bank Conference on Economic Developmer* (Washington, DC.: World Bank), 27–56.

UN–ECE (1998, 2003, 2004) *Economic Survey of Europe* (New York and Geneva: United Nations Economic Commission for Europe).

World Bank (2000) *Making Transition Work for Everyone* (Oxford: Oxford University Press), Appendix D.

World Bank (2004) *Poland: Growth, Employment and Living Standards in Pre-Accession Poland*, Report 28233-Pol (Washington, DC: World Bank), March.

Zak, P. J. and St. Knack (2001) 'Trust and growth', *Economic Journal* 111, 295–321.

2
Two Competing Concepts of Transition

Chapter 2 presents two different intellectual concepts of transition. On the surface, these concepts were initially identified with the debate about 'shock-therapy versus gradualism'. However, the differences were deeper and rooted in different schools of economic thought. Behind the shock approach we find the so-called 'Washington Consensus', which dominated economic policy in transition countries for many years. This approach is based on liberalization, privatization and stabilization as cornerstones of the transition to a market economy. The contributors to this approach shared a deep belief in flexible prices, market transactions, and a minimalist state. The approach is contrasted with the 'evolutionary–institutionalist' concept, which emphasizes the role of informal institutions such as behavior and mindsets as well as formal institutions such as the rule of law. This approach takes into account that institution building is a time-consuming process, in particular when some institutions such as those of the financial sector within the transition countries have to be created from scratch.

The 'Washington Consensus' approach

Shock therapy ...

At the beginning of the 1990s, nobody could safely assume that communist party dictatorship was already a closed chapter in CEE history. The CEE countries had previously experienced periods of weak communist rule, and all attempts to reform the Soviet-style economy in these periods (GDR 1953, Hungary 1956, Czechoslovakia 1968, Poland 1979–81) by implanting more autonomy and financial incentives, among them more flexible prices, into the state-owned enterprises (SOEs) had failed, since the countries were under the strict control of the Soviet Union, who feared a break-up of her empire. Without the Soviet threat of military intervention, Poland's General Jaruzelski would not have imposed martial law in Poland in December 1981 and attempted to stifle reform concepts worked out by economists.[1] In China, the communist party started reforms in 1978 aimed at a socialist market economy, but in 1989 it was not yet quite clear which direction these reforms would actually take. What CEE reformers feared in 1989 was a scenario like the Tiananmen massacre in Peking in June, when the Chinese leadership had used the army to defend the rule of the party. The new political elites in Poland, Czechoslovakia, and, later, Bulgaria and Romania, were convinced that only swift action would break the political and economic basis of the old *nomenklatura* and ensure popular support for the transition to democracy by improving living standards. One may say that the *political issue* of breaking up communist and Soviet rule was looking for a base in economics, and the 'Washington Consensus' provided this base. The prominent example is the Polish reform concept elaborated by the Polish economist Leszek Balcerowicz who, as a communist party member, developed a far-reaching reform concept around 1980, but became completely convinced by martial law that the political system could actually be changed only by the radical elimination of its economic basis.

This concept of economic-based political transition included the almost complete liberalization of prices, trade, and business at one stroke, the rapid privatization of SOEs, and the downsizing of the state's role in society. This concept was called *shock therapy*. The rapid and comprehensive privatization was a prerequisite for the withdrawal of the state from responsibility for the economy in order to break the influence of industrial pressure groups, still linked with the old nomenclature, on the government. Insolvent enterprises, which could not be sold, should be immediately closed. Most members of the new elite shared a gloomy view of the heritage of the socialist system: an outdated stock of physical capital producing 'useless output' due to long-lasting 'overinvestment'. This 'scrap hypothesis' (Sinn and Sinn, 1994) was popular among many economists. An apt metaphor for the 'shock' idea is: 'Centrally planned and market economies are like two territories separated by a deep river. This river can be got over only by one leap. A step-by-step crossing will end in drowning.'

... plus price stabilization

The 'Washington Consensus' approach (Box 2.1) relates to the specific combination of shock-like transition and macroeconomic stabilization. 'Stabilization' was meant to achieve price stability as a prerequisite for (long-term) growth. The 'Washington Consensus' was a paradigm in the Washington-based institutions the IMF and the World Bank and some American think tanks to solve the structural balance of payment

---

Box 2.1 The 'Washington Consensus'

John Williamson coined the phrase 'Washington Consensus' in 1990, 'to refer to the lowest common denominator of policy advice being addressed by the Washington-based institutions to Latin American countries as of 1989' (Williamson 2000). These policies were:

- Fiscal discipline (a redirection of public expenditure priorities toward fields offering both high economic returns and the potential to improve income distribution – such as primary health care, primary education, and infrastructure)
- Tax reform (to lower marginal rates and broaden the tax base)
- Interest rate liberalization
- A competitive exchange rate
- Trade liberalization
- Liberalization of inflows of foreign direct investment (FDI)
- Privatization
- Deregulation (to abolish barriers to entry and exit)
- Secure property rights

The phrase 'Washington Consensus' became a lightning rod for dissatisfaction among anti-globalization protestors, developing country politicians and officials, trade negotiators, and numerous others. Apart from its political relevance, the Consensus was rooted in the then mainstream economics, which could be found in macroeconomic and microeconomic text books, and which had a strong commitment to neoclassical economics, supply-side economics, monetarism, and the theory of rational expectations. The unexpected breakdown of real output, the emergence of stubborn unemployment and poverty in transition countries and in Asian and Latin American countries applying the recipes of the 'Washington Consensus' gave cause for ongoing debate and analysis among economists. The initial content of the 'Washington Consensus' eroded in the face of this debate. An 'augmented' Consensus (Rodrik 2001) seems today[1] to include corporate governance anti-corruption policy, flexible labour markets, WTO agreements (of controlled external opening), financial codes and standards for stabilizing the financial sector, 'prudent' capital account opening (= gradual liberalization), either a floating exchange rate or a currency board), independent central banks + inflation targeting (in contrast to financial programming), social safety nets, and targeted poverty reduction.

[1]Global Trade Negotiations Home Page, Center for International Development at Harvard University; available at http://www.cid.harvard.edu/cidtrade/issues/washington.html.

---

problems of underdeveloped and newly industrialized countries (NICs) (prominently in Latin America), and the problem of hyperinflation. The diagnosis of hyperinflation in Latin America in the 1980s focused on populist governments, which tried to find electoral support by extensive expenditure programmes and high fiscal deficits. Most socialist economies suffered from severe macroeconomic imbalances: a mismatch between supply and demand, trade deficits, and high foreign debt – a further gloomy legacy for the transition. These imbalances were explained as being the combination of price controls and government subsidies to state enterprises, yielding no visible real economic effect, but being financed through the printing of money by the National Bank, serving as a government agency. With demand always higher than potential output, commodities vanished from official markets and were traded on black markets at uncontrolled higher prices. The lifting of price controls without the abolition of the causes of imbalance might lead instead to hyperinflation,[2] as in Latin America, and make the free price system ineffective. David Lipton *and* Jeffrey Sachs (1990) presented a widely accepted model that demonstrated why price liberalization and stabilization policy should stand prominently at the beginning of the transition and why both were so closely tied to each other (see the Appendix 1, p. 36).

The first step of macroeconomic policy was to transform the politically dependent National Bank into an *independent central bank*. Secondly, the money supply was intended to be controlled by *financial programming*. If direct credit of the central bank to the government was forbidden, and money was held short, the government would be forced to avoid fiscal deficits. Aggregate demand would be cut by its excess component and fall to the level of potential output. The instruments to achieve this goal were the control of the money supply (sometimes coupled with a currency reform), high nominal interest rates exceeding the rate of inflation (= a high real interest rate), and a competitive exchange rate. The elimination of excess demand would not seriously harm output and employment. A 'transitional recession' could be expected for a period of about a year, not exceeding some 5 per cent, which was accepted in facilitating changes to price relativities.

The evolutionary–institutionalist approach

Gradualism ...

The counter-project to the 'Washington Consensus' emerged over time and was rooted in many branches of heterodox schools of economic thought. Their critical contribution to the transition debate has a common link to the evolutionary–institutional perspective of social systems including the market economy; Gérard Roland (2001) coined the term 'evolutionary–institutionalist' approach.

Initially, shock therapy was opposed by the gradualist approach, which opposed the necessity of price liberalization and the possibility of rapid privatization. 'Gradualists' recommended an adequate sequencing of reform steps to allow individuals and organizations to adjust their behaviour. The main argument against sudden price liberalization was that price signals imply a competitive environment (Gabrisch and Laski 1990); if this environment did not exist some form of price controls might prove to be superior to simple price liberalization. The support for competition would be more important than quick mass privatization. Gradualists had a more balanced perspective on the heritage of the socialist past. Even the worst SOE disposed of a certain amount of information, which could be useful and even indispensable during the transition. The destruction of the society's capital might turn the *nomenklatura* into a mafia. Controversies over the 'Washington Consensus' approach existed also in other fields, among them over stabilization issues.

The evolutionary perspective borrows from information theory. According to Peter Murrell (Murrell 1993), the leading question is how societies can efficiently use the knowledge available to them and how socioeconomic processes can preserve and enhance the knowledge that exists in society. Organizations need time to adjust to new conditions to change their behaviour. Murrell's metaphor (1993, p. 220) applied to the transition is as follows: 'Societies can be compared to climbers trying to find the top of hill enveloped in cloud. With limited information on the local topography, the best they can do is to take the path of steepest ascent and to move forward in small steps, reevaluating their information at each stage.'

The institutional perspective has roots in the long history of institutional economics (for an overview, see Klein 1999). With respect to transition, it is closely related to the *informational problem* of modern societies underlined by gradualists. Institutionalists who argued that a functioning market economy consists in more than flexible prices and a minimal state. Only institutions make free prices work, for they provide the reliable information necessary for prices to reflect both expectations and scarce resources. A shock-like transition upsets a given system of expectations and economically founded expectations cannot longer be formulated. Prices lose their role as a reliable guide for decisions. This is the reason why 1972 Nobel Prize Winner Kenneth J. Arrow (Arrow 2000) dubbed free market prices in the shock-like transition as 'unfair', particularly the prices of enterprises in the privatization process. The price of a whole enterprise or of its shares on the capital market, reflects the expectations about, its future profitability. A fair assessment is not possible when the enterprise holds a monopoly position in the production chain in the socialist economy and is mostly capital-intensive. Institution building is crucial for the reduction of uncertainty.

... plus crisis prevention

Gradualists were less concerned with the destructive impact of a possible hyperinflation, but rather with the absence of *institutional stability*. Behind the hyperinflation threat they saw not inherited demand-pull factors such as permanent deficit spending but a cost-push cause such as the steep increase of oil and energy prices and a sharp devaluation (affecting the domestic price of imported raw materials and intermediate goods). Price controls, including wages and the exchange rate, should therefore be applied until the money overhang had been eliminated and the threat of a price–wage spiral had vanished (Gabrisch and Laski 1990). The AGENDA group (Jan Kregel, Egon Matzner, and Gernot Grabher; see Kregel, Matzner, and Grabher, 1992 – the group included also Amit Bhaduri and Kazimierz Laski) related its critique to the destructive impact Keynes ascribed to *uncertainty* in a monetary production economy. Holding back money rather than making investment is a typical reaction of agents to defend against uncertainty, the AGENDA group argued that institutions reduce uncertainty, for they tend to introduce a degree of regularity and predictability into both individual and collective behaviour. Keynesians were concerned with the decrease in aggregate demand and employment caused by tough fiscal and monetary policies. While the advocates of the 'Washington Consensus' predicted a quick recovery of the economy and growth, the AGENDA group argued that the result of a shock-like transition combined with macroeconomic stabilization would be unpredictable. Monetary Keynesians argued that IMF-style stabilization would establish the shortage function of money, but high interest rates would prevent the establishment of the asset function of money, which is equally important for an investment dynamic (Riese 1992).

In contrast to the 'Washington Consensus' stabilization concept, the evolutionary–institutional approach linked the problem of price stabilization with the development of credit and money relations, particularly concerning the effects on real output, employment, and income distribution. The development of proper institutions should include: law enforcement, sufficient capacities of the central bank to supervise the banking sector, or well-established corporate governance schemes relating the financial and non-financial sectors of the economy. The proposal included also the protection of some collateral for private households (a flat, or shares in privatized enterprises, or money savings) and small enterprises. Money savings could be protected by the renunciation of a confiscatory currency reform or the avoidance of a 'corrective inflation'. The inherited monetary overhang should be changed into illiquid assets to be used as collateral for investment credits.

Financial stability

A relevant case for the institutionalist argument was provided by the financial crises in South East Asia and Latin America in the 1990s. These crisis confronted an IMF-style stabilization policy (high interest rates, a fixed exchange rate, expenditure cuts) with the institutional constraints in the financial sector, above all the *corporate governance* problem. From an institutional perspective, a market economy is based on financial contracts between the owner of a financial asset and the debtor, which are charged over time. This constitutes a *commitment problem* between the creditor and the debtor: The creditor can never be absolutely certain that a debtor is willing or able to repay (Eichengreen and Hausmann 1999). With a shock-like increase of interest rates or with cuts in the money supply and restricted access to bank credit (a 'credit crunch'), debtors would not be able to repay and enterprises would not be able get credits for financing new equipment, labour, and raw material. The chain of financial contracts in the economy would break down and immediately lead to a financial crisis, with severe results for income distribution to the poorer households. The problem would become more severe in transition countries, where law enforcement and corporate governance were weak, where there was a lack of collateral for credit, and where the central bank had no capacity to supervise the banking sector. These were important causes of the financial crises that hit Bulgaria and Romania in 1995–97, the Czech Republic in May 1997, and Russia in August 1998. Providing stability in the financial sector of the economy is one of the shared beliefs of Keynesians and institutionalists in their view of a systemic transition, and both see here a major role for an active government.

Fundamental differences in transitional issues

The advocates of both the shock-therapy and the 'Washington Consensus' shared a deep belief in the positive role of flexible prices and open markets for rationality and efficiency, and a deep mistrust of government intervention. The leading question behind the belief in this kind of economics reads: how should we *rationalize the actions* of individual agents? The evolutionary–institutionalist view asks how human beings gain control over their lives by developing a structure to order their relationship with the environment (Nobel Prize Winner Douglass C. North, see North 2003). While the 'Washington Consensus' assumes that rationality is the basis for growth and welfare, the evolutionary–institutionalist view adds an institutional structure to the determinants of growth. From this fundamental difference in the perspective on society and its economy have stemmed many disagreements about the transition to a market economy (see Table 2.1).

Table 2.1 Fundamental differences between the 'Washington Consensus' and the evolutionary–institutional approaches

	'Washington Consensus'	Evolutionary–institutional approach
Images	'Get over a deep river by one leap': Shock-like liberalization, macroeconomic stabilization, and downsizing the state	'Build a bridge between both banks of the river': gradual and sequenced actions including institution building, competition, support for private business, solving the corporate governance problem
Initial conditions	The legacy is a burden and represents 'old' and inefficient connections, more *nomenklatura* than market; choose the first-best 'socially engineered' solution that is not 'distorted' by the initial condition	The heritage has a value that should be protected; otherwise the destruction of the society's social capital changes the *nomenklatura* into a mafia
Attitude towards SOEs	Privatize quickly in order to avoid asset-stripping and rent-seeking; close down inefficient enterprises	Gradual downsizing relying on the development of the private sector
Prices	Flexible prices on free markets lead to efficiency and growth; they signal expectations and ensure rational behaviour	Institutions ensure stable expectations, and prices are only one institution among others; flexible prices are unfair during transition
Macro-economic policy	Price stabilization through control of the money supply, cut government expenditure, introduce nominal wage and exchange rate anchors	Output stabilization; hence control of the real-economy effects of stabilization, above all unemployment
The leading question	How to rationalize actions of individual agents = producers and consumers	How human beings gain control over their lives by developing a structure to order their relationship to the environment (North 2003)

Continued

Table 2.1   (Continued)

	'Washington Consensus'	Evolutionary–institutional approach
Predict-ability	With rationalized behaviour and under a given legal environment = results of individual actions are predictable as well as the result of transition	With free entry and exit of markets and technological progress the institutional environment changes, and results of individual and collective actions are not predictable, as well of as the results transition
Transactions in a market economy	Only market transactions are efficient	Market and non-market transactions contribute to efficiency; do not neglect social relations including corporate governance
Property rights	Physical ownership of assets	Ownership + right to contract + control of contract fulfilment
State and government	Minimal state; downsize the state's share in GDP and in employment	Reform the state and use it for law enforcement and to secure property rights; pro-poor and crisis-prevention policy in order to support the middle classes

Predictability

Both the questions above lead to different statements about the *predictability* of individual action, and of the result of transition. Individual agents learn by repeated actions, although they make mistakes, the price mechanism makes them adjust and rationalize their behaviour. With flexible prices, the result of transition would also be predictable. The best and shortest concept of transition would be the import of the constitution of a real existing market economy. This is the reason, why the shock-therapy approach is sometimes called the 'social engineering' approach, because politicians could engineer the first-best social solution that was not distorted by the inherited burden. The evolutionary–institutionalist approach relies on *uncertainty*, which is generally caused by technological change and open markets, and specifically caused by the transition of institutions. The result of transition thus cannot be predicted.

Market and non-market transactions

The 'Washington Consensus' focuses on market transactions guided by flexible prices. The firm has a calculable value only via market transactions. Getting the prices right is the approach to evaluating the market value of firms. The evolutionary–institutionalist view explains the success of market economies by the combination of market and non-market transactions. Firms are *social institutions* with an intra-firm exchange of services and goods. This exchange is based on the the formal organization of the firm and on conventions and implicit contracts (for example, to behave cooperatively as a member of the organization, or to have a corporate identity). The size of non-market transactions inside a firm grows with the growing complexity of the firm. Also, growing and competing firms try to develop networks of companies, devoted to an exchange of goods and services outside the open and free market and at non-market prices (intra-firm prices, for example). Seen from this perspective, a socialist firm needs to be evaluated by more than market prices.

Property rights

In the 'Washington Consensus' view on transition, the term 'property rights' had a focus on the physical ownership of assets plus guarantees against state expropriation (= nationalization). Therefore, ownership in the transition should create clearly defined property rights. Institutionalists underlined the fact that the simple issue of ownership does not generate the unambiguous individual rights needed for a successful market economy. Property rights include also the right to contract and to control the contract (Kregel Matzner, and Drabher 1992) Lacking law enforcement and control rights, private ownership would always be threatened by private expropriatation (see Djankov *et al.* 2003) through the non-fulfilment of contractual obligations, or even robbery.

Corporate governance

An important non-market transaction inside a firm, relevant for privatization and the restructuring of firms during transition, is *corporate governance* (Box 2.2) – that is the institutional set for controlling managers ('agents')

Box 2.2 Corporate governance

Corporate governance is the system by which business corporations are directed and controlled. The corporate governance structure specifies the distribution of rights and responsibilities among different participants in the corporation, such as the board, managers, shareholders and other stakeholders, and spells out the rules and procedures for making decisions on corporate affairs. By doing this, it also provides the structure through which the company objectives are set, and the means of attaining those objectives and monitoring performance (OECD 1999).

---

by owners (the 'principal') – a problem also closely related to the property rights issue, for it defines the *rights of control* inside a firm.

The 'Washington Consensus' approach to transition understated this issue, while in the literature the corporate governance problem was identified relatively early as being of particular relevance in a transition economy. Phelps *et al.* (1993) argued that the formerly communist countries ran the risk of creating a mutant system that could not come close to matching the efficiency and dynamism of a normal capitalist system:

> Instituting a price system through the decentralisation of resource allocation and the deregulation of enterprises, and instituting private enterprise through legalisation of private share-owning and mass privatisation, are necessary but far from sufficient to achieve the potential of a capitalist market economy.

The argument is simply based on a restructuring of state-owned and privatized firms, and for that sound corporate governance is a prerequisite.

The transformational role of the state

A cornerstone of the 'Washington Consensus' was the idea of the interventionist state as a weak state, being the victim of industrial pressure groups, lobbies, and social movements (see, for example, Balcerowicz 1995, 1997). The possible resort of a populist government to new expenditure programmes and structural policies was seen to be a typical outcome of a weak state, and would only offer new occasions for *rent-seeking* (Box 2.3). Only decisive actions by a reformist government could keep these populist pressures in check. The strong state in transition was seen as an 'autonomous' agent, able to implement and capable of managing the

---

Box 2.3   Rent-seeking

The great British economist David Ricardo (1772–1823) coined the term 'rent'. In his historically narrow sense, a rentier holds a resource (land, for example) the quantity of which cannot be increased or obtained from others and hence, exacts a rent for its use. The American economist Anne Krueger invented the term 'rent-seeking' in 1974. Rent-seeking behaviour is a phenomenon in countries with mixed economies in which government intervention is extensive. It aims at avoiding competitive or market pressure in order to bring about price distortions in one's own interest in the political sphere. Rent-seeking describes how agents aim to avoid competitive or market pressure by creating price distortions in their own interest in the political sphere. Rent-seeking is extensively linked with corruption of politicians and bureaucrats.

various steps of transition without other input from the society than general elections each four or to years – and at best in form of a majority voting system to ensure clear political majorities (Lipton and Sachs 1990). The dominance of rapid privatization over the designing of appropriate competition policy rules (regulating competition) was a typical facet of this thinking. The reformist governments of some countries also disowned responsibility for the SOEs in the initial stages of transition.

In the evolutionary–institutionalist view, the state has a guiding role in producing markets, in law enforcement, in securing property rights, and in pro-poor and crisis-prevention policy in order to support the middle classes. From economic theory's point of view, the state produces *positive externalities* to the private sector and mitigates the effect of *negative externalities* (Laski and Bhaduri 1997). Institutionalists argue that modern market economies all over the world are *mixed economies* consisting of a public sector (with SOEs) and a private sector (with some state shares). Both sectors are more or less in an equilibrium of complementarities. For example, investment into the public infrastructure promises better profitability for many private investors. The stabilisation of wage costs, aggregate demand, and financial sector stability are other examples of external economies that an active government can provide to the private sector. One can say that both the private and the public sectors are in a kind of mutual symbiosis, and that this principle holds also for the transition countries (see Bhaduri 1994). Too rapid a speed of transition can destroy profit opportunities for the emerging private sector, in particular the emerging middle classes. From this results a field for intervention, when collective action might harm the economy (a bank run, for example). For these tasks, the state needs reform and not destruction. Where there is a positive heritage of the past, this should be defended and developed by restructuring (of SOEs) and structural policy, following the successful patterns of Japan, South Korea, Taiwan, and other NICs (Amsden, Kochanowicz, and Taylor 1994).

The dispute over stabilization policy

Inflation as a legacy from central planning

All CEE countries started their transition with high and still suppressed inflation (many prices were controlled in the planned economy). The Lipton–Sachs model (1990, see Appendix, p. 36) demonstrates how price liberalization initially leads to the once-and-for-all elimination of the stock of excess demand accumulated over many years of controlled prices. This move from suppressed to open inflation was later named 'corrective inflation'. Lipton and Sachs identified state subsidies above all as the source of suppressed inflation financing the waste of resources. However, since free prices do not automatically mean the absence of state subsidies, inflation may continue, and above all, fiscal balances need to be got right. The model excludes any effect of stabilization policy on output and employment, an assumption, highly disputed between the two attitudes to transition.

Apart from the theoretical model, the IMF's stabilization policy recommendations were rooted in various fears about uncontrolled inflation, above all about inflationary expectations. Stabilization policy here includes more than fiscal policy. In transition countries, the complete change in the institutional framework may contribute to high inflationary expectations:

(1) Workers may understand the corrective inflation not as a temporary phenomenon, curbing only excess real wages, but rather as a real decline of their purchasing power. They may react by demanding higher nominal wages (= cost inflation).

(2) SOEs may react to the expected cut in state subsidies with higher prices on monopolistic markets.

(3) If confidence in the stability of domestic currency is losing ground, financial contracts will be written more and more in foreign currency ('dollarization'), and the velocity of money will soar.

The major aim of stabilization policy was to eliminate the sources of excess demand, to stabilize inflationary expectations in order to avoid the emergence of hyperinflation, and to strengthen the functions of the domestic currency.

The financial programming of the IMF and the Keynesian critique

From the IMF's point of view, inflation was based upon an actual increase of money and credit and of the velocity of money circulation under the condition of supply rigidity. The former was a problem of monetary policy of the central bank that accommodated the various requirements of the non-financial sector, the latter was a problem of inflationary expectations of firms, private households, and workers. But how to design stabilization policy in an economy, where legal money had not previously played a key role, and a black money market was spread throughout the economy ('dollarization')? The functions of money were weak, the transmission channels for a typical stabilization policy in market economies – the interest rate, open market operations, etc. – were ineffective, and currency competition (domestic versus foreign currency) was threatened. The IMF offered *financial programming*, a concept based mainly on the use of quantitative tools – that is the printing of central bank money and credit for the non-financial sector (see Appendix 2). The starting point for IMF policy recommendations was to create an independent central bank and then control the money supply.

The Keynesian critique focused on the crucial assumptions of the IMF concept: a constant velocity of money, unexpected adjustment processes, and of fixed output in the short run.

Velocity of money

The starting point of emerging market economies with a small and weak financial sector and money functions might be a very low velocity. A reduction in money supply does not lead automatically to less inflation, it could lead to higher velocity of money when inflationary expectations are very high and agents can index their financial contracts. Conversely, an expansion of money supply does not necessarily lead to more inflation, it could lead to a higher monetization of the economy.

Unexpected adjustments

The restriction of credit might also entail unfavourable adjustments on the same side – for example, improve the trade balance so strongly that even higher inflation would result. Also, inflation might be reduced so much to permit an even a higher trade deficit. Therefore, the IMF stabilization package included a devaluation of the currency in order to ensure a surplus in the trade balance. However, a devaluation would yield the expected results only when the Marshall–Lerner condition that the sum of export and import elasticity needs to be larger than 1 – is fulfilled, an uncertain assumption (see also Chapter 6).

The IMF stabilization package based on financial programming plus some flanking measure such as a devaluation is also named 'orthodox' stabilization. Because of the unknown links between a devaluation of the price level or of the wage demands of workers, some countries – among them, most transition countries – introduced some additional measures such as wage controls or fixed exchange rates (after devaluation), or so-called 'heterodox' programmes. These controls have the functions of nominal 'anchors'. A fixed exchange rate links domestic expectations on inflation with the inflation of the anchor currency (in most cases, the US dollar or a trade-weighted basket of currencies). Other stabilization programmes even included some control of commodity prices.

Fixed output

Imagine an emerging private sector with weak financial equipment, solely dependent on expected own profits which, however, are the future results of actual investment in fixed capital and working capital. A monetary restriction will limit the chances for expanding the private sector. Current production in SOEs might also be hampered, for working capital (= finance for inputs) becomes very expensive. In general, a shock-like increase in interest rates or cuts in the money supply and restricted access to bank credit means that debtors will not be able to repay and enterprises will not be able get credit to finance new equipment, labour, and raw materials (a 'credit crunch').

The shortcomings of fiscal retrenchment

Another critical point is the impact of fiscal retrenchment on aggregate demand. Obviously, financial programming disregarded the income multiplier effects completely: A lower real public expenditure would reduce aggregate demand by more than the initial contraction. The cumulative effect includes also effects on the second and third rounds of the adjustment process. An uncalculable effect is the erosion of the tax basis: less expenditures leads to less revenues, and the budget cannot be so easily balanced.

The 'Washington Consensus' advocated a more effective tax system. Two major problems emerged: tax evasion and weak tax collection. Mitra and Stern (2002) provide four arguments for tax evasion rooted in the 'post-socialist legacy':

- A culture of *mutual mistrust* between taxpayers and tax authorities
- No tradition of *voluntary compliance* with tax legislation
- No tradition of *appeals to the courts* against the decision of the tax authorities which, by enhancing trust in the fairness of the tax administration, would encourage voluntary compliance
- No tradition of *self-assessment*, which would shift the burden of appraisal to the private sector and reduce the administrative demands placed on the tax authorities.

Weak tax collection in transition countries has three causes:

- The *tax authorities* had to be established. The capacity of the tax authorities was very small at the beginning of transition.
- Tax collection seems to depend on a *stable tax system*. In countries with frequent changes in taxation, tax collection is less effective.
- It seems to be that the ability to collect taxes shrinks with the *value added tax* (VAT) introduced early in most countries. VAT is a rather

complicated tax and needs a special bureaucratic procedure for companies.

Attempts to balance the budget were threatened by a fall in tax revenues. Following financial programming, frequent expenditure cuts were necessary, but worsened the aggregate demand problem during transition.

A country taxonomy of transition

The transition on 30 June of the GDR presented the unique occasion to study the 'social engineering' idea in practice: the GDR citizens went to bed on 30 June 1990 in a socialist economy and woke up on the next day in the market economy of West Germany. The specific feature of the GDR – East German transition is the complete absence of a GDR monetary policy and the presence of the 'rich brother', West Germany, whose tax payers took over most of the transaction costs of transition and provided the money to sustain it. Fiscal policy in East Germany is thus a reflection of transfers from federal budgets and West German *Länder* budgets. East Germany is a transfer economy, where transfers have the function of a macroeconomic 'soft' budget constraint.

The taxonomy of the remaining CEE countries according to both approaches is more difficult, because the transition had the character of a stop–go cycle. Elements of shock-like policy were mixed or replaced by more gradualist programmes. Hungary and Slovenia afforded more gradualism than other countries. Hungary's opening up and structural reform process went back to 1968. Price liberalization was not a matter of hot debate, for price reforms had led to prices already quite close to world market prices. Unlike other countries (Poland, for example), the political elite of both countries was not inclined to accept western advice (from the IMF and related organizations, nor from their opponents), for they had been an economy for a long time open, and its economists had engaged in the international scientific community.

In Poland, the first country to launch shock therapy in 1990, new governments were committed to soften the transition shocks after democratic elections, causing the emergence of a populist policy. Financial programming played a major role in stabilization policy in the early stages of transition. This course of events seems also to have held for Slovakia and Romania. In the Czech Republic and the Baltic countries the Washington Consensus recipes were more consistently applied.

The CIS countries followed a path of an authoritarian state, particularly in the Central Asian countries, in Belarus and, until 2004, in the Ukraine. In Belarus and the Central Asian countries there is little evidence on transition, either as a gradual or a shock-like concept. Russia is somewhat different: the Gajdar reforms of 1992 were cousins of the 'Washington Consensus' approach; however, they failed as they created huge opportunities for rent-seeking and ended in an oligarchic society. Political unrest prevented a restrictive monetary and fiscal policy but there was high inflation and an output collapse. The new reform approach under president Putin has followed a more evolutionary concept.

China is different again. First, it is perhaps gradualist approach with few attraction for gradualists, for three reasons: lacking democracy, the mixture of transition with development problems, and the country's size that lowered the necessity for thorough-going trade openness. As a less-developed economy, China had other problems and opportunities for growth. While transition in the CEE countries, and in particular in the later EU member countries, was a matter of restructuring industry, in China it was a problem of organizing the transition of an agricultural society into an industrial one. A typical sign of successful developing countries is the creation of industrial employment for large village populations. This is a prerequisite for high output. The interesting point, however, is that the Chinese authorities never attempted to choke off real growth by achieving a zero inflation rate, although they tried to prevent too high inflation.

Appendix 1: the Lipton–Sachs model of combining liberalization and stabilization

Assume an economy producing and consuming a single good with a fixed nominal price P, and a fixed output S. Nominal income (and demand) Y is exogenously given. Monetary equilibrium at the official market is given with $Y = PS$. If Y were smaller than PS, the economy were demand constrained. The rationing mechanism is P. Where Y is greater than PS, excess demand (ex) emerges and can be measured as a percentage of nominal demand:

$$ex = (Y-PS)/Y \tag{2A1.1}$$

With excess demand, consumers are not able to buy a certain amount of the good without waiting in a line. The rationing mechanism is now the waiting time q. The model assumes that 'middlemen' or arbitrageurs purchase the entire output at the official price and sell it at a black market price P_b. The nominal equilibrium in the economy is then given at $Y = P_b S$. ($P_b - P$) represents the nominal profit of the middlemen from waiting. The real profit $(P_b - P)/P_b$ compensates for the loss of utility from waiting.

All individuals have a simple utility function:

$$U = C + wL \tag{2A1.2}$$

where C is consumption of the good, and L is leisure. The variable w represents the marginal utility of leisure. The maximum amount of time for leisure is N (in hours). The time worked is fixed, because output is also fixed. Waiting in the line reduces the leisure time available below its maximum value N. Total leisure time is then

$$L = N - qS \qquad (2A1.3)$$

Without excess demand, q would be 0, and L equals N. The entry to the black market is free, and new arbitrageurs would enter so long the real profit compensates for the loss of utility due to the fall in leisure time. When the real profit equals the marginal utility of leisure, arbitrage comes to an end:

$$w = (P_b - P)/P_b q \qquad (2A1.4)$$
$$P_b = P/(1 - wq). \qquad (2A1.4a)$$

Since each unit of the good is sold on the black market, monetary equilibrium in the economy is given by the condition $P_b S = Y$. So we obtain

$$Y = PS(1 - wq) \qquad (2A1.5)$$
$$q = ((Y - PS))/wY = ex/w. \qquad (2A1.6)$$

The amount of waiting time is directly proportional to the percentage of excess demand in the economy. Taking (2A1.6) and (2A1.3), we can determine the utility level:

$$U = C + w(N - exS/w). \qquad (2A1.7)$$

Because consumption equals the supply of the good, we write:

$$U = S(1 - ex) + wN. \qquad (2A1.8)$$

Equation (2A1.8) reveals that excess demand is costly because it leads to activities that consume real resources. The equation illustrates a situation where the costs of 'rent-seeking' behaviour emerge. What is more: when official real income Y/P is reduced to the level of S, utility will increase, for the time for leisure

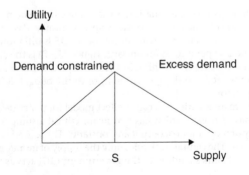

Figure 2A1.1 Utility and real income

increases. Utility will fall in a situation when the real income is reduced in a demand-constrained situation ($Y/P \leq S$) (see also Figure 2A1.1).

Excess demand can be eliminated by abolishing the price controls and by curbing nominal income. In the first case, P would adjust upwards and balance supply and demand ('corrective inflation'). The elimination of all sources of excess demand in the current year would stabilize the free price at the given level ('stabilization'). An increase of Y in subsequent years, however, would again generate excess demand and, with free prices, turn into inflation.

The problem with this model is aggregation. The model starts – like microeconomics – with one single market and assumes simply that all single markets in the economy possess the same characteristics. It is impossible to aggregate the divergent utility functions of millions of individuals. In addition, it is almost impossible to aggregate the net effect of the size and scope of excess demand for single goods in an economy. Excess demand for one good does not automatically mean excess demand for all goods. In the CPE, there were many goods whose prices were fixed at a level to suppress demand. Abandoning controlled prices means that prices of some goods – mainly so-called 'luxury goods' – decline while other prices – mainly basic consumer goods – tend to increase. Whether the aggregate level of utility will increase depends not only on the simple increase in the price level, but also on changes in the consumer (or investment) goods basket.

Appendix 2: IMF financial programming

This concept goes back to Polak's model (Polak 1957) for developing countries with a weak financial sector in the economy. Financial programming is based on the double entry accounts of external trade and banking. The liabilities of the financial sector (money supply Ms[3]) are matched by the assets held by that sector: international reserves and credit to the private sector plus credit to the government. While the technical side of the model, based on some macroeconomic identities, is more or less undisputed, the underpinning with monetarist theory is far from being so (Bhaduri, 1992).

The basic macroeconomic identity in financial programming is

$$\Delta kPX + kP\Delta X + kX\Delta P \equiv (E-Z) + F + \Delta B + \Delta G \qquad (2A2.1)$$

where the left-hand side of the equation is the change in the demand for money, and the right-hand side the change in the supply of money. P is the price level, k is the velocity of money, and X is real output, hence ΔP is inflation. E is revenues from exports, and Z expenditures for imports. Hence, $(E-Z)$ is the change in international reserves from trade. To this add the net capital inflow F. A change of G corresponds to the credit to the government, or to the budget deficit. B is credit to the banking sector.

The change from an identity to a cause–effect model for policy design is made by the *quantity theory of money*, which has two major critical assumptions: the first is that the velocity of money and of output are constants. The second is the exogenous character of money. The central bank rules only the supply of money in an economy. That is, the central bank's lending to the government (ΔG) acts as 'high-powered money' – i.e. as a credit base for commercial banks additional lending to the private sector. In this case, one can write: $\Delta B = n\Delta G$, where n is the credit multiplier.

Division of (2A1.9) by the GDP (PX) leads us to the basis for financial programming:

$$k\frac{\Delta P}{P} + C = \frac{(E - Z)}{PX} + \frac{F}{PX} + (1 + n)\frac{\Delta G}{PX}$$

where $C = \Delta k + \Delta X/X$ is zero by assumption.

A reduction of credit to the government (or of the share of the budget deficit in GDP) results either in lower inflation ($\Delta P/P$) or in the improvement of the trade balance in terms of GDP. Credit programming was a quantitative approach in the first stage of transition, and the main tools were the control of money printing and the interest rate.

Notes

1. Hungary had been an astonishing exception since the 1970s, characterized by price reforms bringing domestic price relations closer to world market prices and by the increasing autonomy of managers (see Chapter 9).
2. Hyperinflation is technically defined as a 50 per cent increase per month in consumer prices against the previous month.
3. We disregard various money concepts, which are introduced and explained in Chapter 3. One could say that 'base money' is the closest concept to financial programming.

References and further reading

Amsden, A., J. Kochanowicz and L. Taylor (1994) *The Market Meets its Match: Restructuring the Economies of Eastern Europe* (Cambridge, MA: Harvard University Press).

Arrow, K. J. (2000) 'Economic transition: speed and scope,' *Journal of Institutional and Theoretical Economics* 156, 9–18.

Balcerowicz, L. (1995) *Socialism, Capitalism, Transformation* (Budapest, London, and New York: Central European University Press (1997).

Balcerowicz, L. (1997) 'The interplay between economic and political transition', in Salvatore Zecchini (ed.), *Lessons from the Economic Transition: Central and Eastern Europe in the 1990s* (London: Kluwer Academic Publishers), 153–169.

Bhaduri, A. (1992) 'Conventional stabilization and the East European transition', in Sandor Richter (ed.), *The Transition from Command to Market Economies in East-Central Europe* (Boulder, CO: Westview Press), 13–51.

Bhaduri, A. (1994) 'Patterns of economic transition and structural adjustments', WIIW-Working Papers 2.

Borenstein, E. R. and J. D. Ostry (1992) 'Structural and macroeconomic determinants of the output decline in Poland: 1990–91', IMF *Working Paper* 92/86.

Djankov, S., E. Glaeser, R. La Porta, F. Lopez-de-Silanes and A. Shleifer (2003) 'The new comparative economics', *Journal of Comparative Economics* 31, 595–619.

Eichengreen, B. and R. Hausman (1999) 'Exchange rates and financial fragility', NBER *Working Paper* 7418.

Gabrisch, H. and K. Laski (1990) 'Transition from the command to a market economy', *WIIW-Research Report* 163 (Vienna: The Vienna Institute for Comparative Economic Studies).

Kiguel, M. A. and N. Liviatan (1992) 'When do heterodox stabilization programs work? Lessons from Experience', *World Bank Research Observer* 7, 35–57.

Klein, P. G. (1999) 'New institutional economics', in B. Bouckaert, G. Boudewijn and De Geest Gervit (eds), *Encyclopedia of Law and Economics* (Northampton, MA: Edgar Elgar), vol. I, 456–489.

Kregel, J. E. Matzner and G. Drabher (eds) (1992) *The Market Shock: An Agenda for the Economic and Social Reconstruction of Central and Eastern Europe* (Vienna: Austrian Academy of Science).

Krueger, A. O. 'The political economy of the rent-seeking society', *American Economic Review* 64, 291–303.

Laski, K. and A. Bhaduri (1997) 'Lessons to be drawn from main mistakes in the transition strategy', in S. Zecchini (ed.), *Lessons from the Economic Transition: Central and Eastern Europe in the 1990s* (London: Kluwer Academic Publishers), 103–122.

Lipton, D. and J. Sachs (1990) 'Creating a market economy in eastern Europe: the case of Poland', *Brookings Papers on Economic Activity* 1990/1, 75–147.

Mencinger, J. (2004) 'Transition to a national and a market economy: a gradualist approach', in M., Mrak, M. Rojec and C. Silva-Jáuregui (eds), *Slovenia: From Yugoslavia to the European Union* (Washington, DC: World Bank), 67–83.

Mickiewicz, T. (2005) *Economic Transition in Central Europe and the Commonwealth of Independent States* (Basingstoke: Palgrave).

Mitra, P., and N. Stern (2002) 'Tax systems in transition', World Bank Policy Research Working Paper 2947.

Murrell, Peter (1993) 'Evolutionary and radical approaches to economic reform', in K. Z. Poznanski (ed.), *Stabilization and Privatization in Poland* (Boston, Dordrecht, and London: Kluwer Academic Press), 215–33.

North, D. C. (2003) 'Understanding the process of economic change', *Forum Series on the Role of Institutions in Promoting Economic Growth* (Washington, DC: Mercatus Center at George Mason University).

Organisation for Economic Co-operation and Development (OECD) (1999). *OECD Principles of Corporate Governance* (Paris).

Phelps, E. S., R. Frydman, A. Rapaczynski and A. Shleifer (1993) 'Needed mechanisms of corporate governance and finance in Eastern Europe', European Bank for Reconstruction and Development, Working Paper 1, 3.

Polak, J. J. (1957). 'Monetary analysis of income formation and payment problems', IMF *Staff Papers* 6, 1–50.

Putnam, R. D. (2000) *Bowling Alone. The Collapse and Revival of American Community* (New York: Simon Schuster).

Riese, H. (1992) 'Transformationsprozeß und Stabilisierungspolitik', in B. Gahlen, H. Hesse and J. J. Ramser (eds), *Von der Plan- zur Marktwirtschaft. Eine Zwischenbilanz* (Tübingen: Mohr), 129–42.

Rodrik, D. (2001) 'The global governance of trade as if development really mattered' (New York: UNDP), available at http://www.servicesforall.org/html/Governance/Rodrik-Trade%20&%20Development.pdf (6 July 2005).

Roland, G. (2001) 'Ten years after ... transition and economics', IMF Staff Papers 48, Special Issue.

Sinn, G. and H.-W. Sinn (1994) *Jumpstart: The Economic Unification of Germany* (Cambridge, MA: MIT Press).

Williamson, J. (1990) *What Washington Means by Policy Reform in Latin American Adjustment: How Much has Happened* (Washington, DC: Institute for International Economics).

Williamson, J. (2000) 'What should the World Bank think about the Washington Consensus?', *World Bank Research Observer* 15, 251–64.

World Bank (1999) 'What is social capital?', *PovertyNet* (Washington, DC: World Bank); available at http://www.worldbank.org/poverty/scapital/whatsc.htm.

3

Financial Institutions, Stability and Growth

> *Chapter 3 stresses the importance of well-functioning financial systems for economic development in a market economy. It is no exaggeration to claim that the transition countries had to build up their financial institutions from scratch. In the planned economy money had no economic function and had to be re-established in the process of transformation.*

The core of the monetary economy: the central bank

Because of socialist ideology, communist states had no commercial financial sectors and money supply was administered by the government. The economy was organised quite contrary to capitalist systems, in the sense that money was not scarce, but could not buy much. The capitalist system, however, is (as Karl Marx quite subtly observed) characterized by apparently having an enormous wealth of commodities, but which is constrained by scarce money. In continuation of our previous discussion about stabilization we could say that money is the macroeconomic budget constraint of the economic system. On the other hand, money also needs the acceptance of the public. The general public needs to trust that money has a value. We can distinguish the four functions of money in modern market economies shown in Box 3.1.

The central bank has the monopoly over the supply of money, which is reflected by a vertical supply curve, as the amount of money in circulation

---

Box 3.1   The functions of money

1. *Medium of exchange*
   • Money provides a medium for the exchange of goods and services which is more efficient than barter
2. *Unit of account*
   • Money provides a unit in which prices are quoted and accounts are kept
3. *Store of value*
   • Money can be used to make purchases in the future
4. *Standard of deferred payment*
   • Money is a unit of account over time: this enables borrowing and lending

---

is issued by the central bank. The amount of money in circulation is measured in three aggregates:

• M1 comprises the traditional definition of money as a means of payment. It includes currency in circulation plus the checkable deposits in depository institutions (banks and thrifts). Currency in bank vaults and bank deposits at the central bank are not a part of M1, although they are part of the *monetary base*, sometimes designated M0.
• M2 includes M1 and adds retail non-transaction deposits.
• M3 includes M2 and adds wholesale deposits.

This money supply meets the *money demand* of the public and the clearing price on the money market is the rate of interest. There has been a long economic debate on whether or not the central bank is really in control of the money supply, because the equilibrium interest rate does, of course, depend on the money demand. For our purposes, we can simply say that the central bank acts as banker to the commercial banking system, which is also referred to as acting as the lender of last resort (LOLR). Modern central banks are independent from the government.

The newly created central banks in transition countries had to win the trust of the public in order to have their currencies accepted for the functions outlined in Box 3.1. This issue, commonly known as the 'stabilization problem' under the 'Washington Consensus' (see Chapter 2), requires the establishment of a sound institutional set-up which enables the central bank to carry out monetary policy in cooperation with the commercial private sector. While the functional criteria of stabilization – i.e. inflation and the exchange rate – are clear, the prerequisites for winning a reputation is less clear. As a minimum it can safely be stated that by definition such a process needs time. This is particularly crucial under the circumstances of the early years of transition, when inflation was high and the exchange rate deteriorated. Furthermore it remains unlikely that the functions of money in a market economy can be established without the existence of *money and capital markets*. We suggest that the central bank is as a participant in these markets rather than an institution of control, which indeed would refer to the era of planned economies. The idea of financial programming and the perfect control of the money supply by the central bank has not much in common with endogenous money supply in the modern monetary economy. Only very few economists such as Michael Kaser (Kaser 1990) saw this problem, which seems to be obvious today, at the very beginning of transition.

Financial systems as stabilizers

The transition towards a market-type economy has experienced substantial setbacks in economic development through crises in the financial sector. The aim of this chapter is therefore to analyse how the financial sector can contribute to the stability of the transition process rather than causing instability. The emphasis of this chapter is therefore not put on the usual question of how to build an efficient financial system in order to ensure the efficient allocation of savings (see, for example, Buch 1997), but focuses on the possibilities of how the financial sector can promote stability and growth.

Two features are commonly addressed regarding the interrelationship between banking crises and macro-economic volatility. These are, first, legacies from the past and, second, undisciplined bank entry. The area of undisciplined market entry concerns the whole topic of mismanagement, fraud, and other deficiencies of human capital within the financial sector and leads to the issue of effective bank supervision and regulation. In the course of this analysis managerial aspects of banking in transition are only touched on in order to concentrate on the 'legacies of the past'. These legacies – the bad debts within the bank's portfolios – do not reflect any mismanagement, but are a heritage specific to the transition from socialism.

The aim is to advance an understanding of the dilemma that low interest rates are needed for the promotion of growth and high rates of interest are imperative in order to secure macroeconomic stability. If the lending rate is given by this market constellation, a sound financial system can contribute to growth without jeopardizing stability through declining spreads.

Next, we take up the issue of banking crises and macroeconomic instability through a discussion of the anatomy of a typical financial crisis, to show the peculiar importance of the financial sector for 'real' output. The 'legacies of the past' imply a disadvantageous starting position for banking in transition, which is the main cause of the vulnerability of the sector. We then enlarge upon the underlying question of the analysis – not only the financial sector's contribution to stability, but also its contribution to growth as the overall economic aim of the transition process is tackled. We conclude that growth promotion through the financial sector can be expected only with decreasing interest rate spreads.

Based on the analytical considerations about finance and transition, as well as the empirical evidence, we then present the concept of financial fragility. Subsequently a strategy of *'semi*-liberalization' for financial sectors will be proposed. The strategy of temporary protection against foreign competitors is deduced from the bad asset problem, but also concerns the second feature of banking in transition, the matter of 'undisciplined entry'. The *'semi*-liberalization' strategy allows for an infant industry policy to improve the stock of human capital within the banking industry in following the argument for rehabilitation of nominal assets of that very industry. It is argued that *'semi*-liberalization' will tend towards to a Rhenish type of bank-based finance rather than an Anglo-Saxon type of stock market finance. The chapter concludes with a discussion of the primacy of external stabilization as a political imperative and stresses the role of internal finance for investment and growth in the long-run process of transition.

Financial fragility

Eichengreen and Hausmann (1999) derive three hypotheses from the literature explaining financial fragility: *moral hazard, original sin*, and the *commitment problem* (see Box 3.2).

Moral hazard means that agents feel sure that they will be bailed out if they encounter repayment difficulties. Explicit or implicit guarantees prevent them from hedging their foreign exposures against the foreign exchange (FX) risk. A pegged exchange rate is an implicit guarantee given by the central bank, mainly to banks and to the government. The costs of this guarantee are normally outweighed by the gains a pegged exchange rate offers. If moral hazard led to excessive risk-taking by the banking sector, the cost might outweight the gains. The banking sector might expand its balance sheet without being limited by its equity capital. The literature describes overborrowing abroad (McKinnon and Pill 1997) and a lending boom (Krugman 1998) as possible consequences: most of short-term-financed investment is allocated in assets.

Box 3.2   Explaining financial fragility: three hypotheses

• *Moral hazard*
  Moral hazard by agents who borrow abroad is likely when they can expect to be bailed out. 'Bailing out' means the existence of explicit or implicit guarantees given by a third party (the government, or an international institution such as the IMF). Corporations and banks are not forced to hedge their foreign exposures: the result is excessive risk-taking.

• *Original sin*
  A history of high inflation and strong and frequent depreciation undermines confidence in the currency of the borrowing country. The currency is not accepted as international reserve money – that is, lenders do not accept debt in the currency. Banks and corporations are not able to hedge their foreign exposure: the result is a currency and/or maturity mismatch of assets and liabilities.

• *Commitment problem*
  Financial contracts are charged over time. If law enforcement is weak, if there is a lack of collateral, or if the institutional framework is weak, the willingness to repay could be constrained: the result could be high spreads on interest that increase financial fragility.

Increased demand for assets is often constrained by supply (land or stock shares), hence, asset prices rise, the quality of bank assets deteriorates, and lending rates increase. The central bank comes under more and more pressure to put a brake on increasing interest rates. When domestic credit exceeds the amount that trade and real growth can absorb, capital inflows may reverse, and the asset bubble burst. If moral hazard constitutes the main source of financial fragility, then the literature recommends the move to an independent float in order to force agents to hedge risks.

The inability to hedge is often coupled with an open foreign exchange position of banks – that is, foreign liabilities exceed foreign assets. But even with a balanced net foreign exchange position, banks are not automatically safer. Since banks tend to carry over the currency risk on their domestic borrowers by foreign currency loans (FCLs), their foreign position may seem balanced at first glance. The FX risk, however, moves from the banks to the company sector or private households. On the demand side, the non-banking sector may be increasingly attracted by borrowing in foreign currency, since it is a typical feature of original-sin countries that the nominal interest rate on domestic credits is higher than that on foreign credits.

A severe currency mismatch may occur when the stream of income from investment financed by FCLs yields only revenues in domestic currency. The same applies with loans to private households since they earn their income exclusively in domestic currency. With an independent float, depreciation would increase the debt service cost associated with the foreign currency loan. More defaults in the company or private household sector would damage the liquidity position of banks. Although depreciation increases the book value of their assets in domestic currency, the value of liquidation may shrink considerably below the book value when the company sector runs into trouble.

Original-sin problems are the reason why central banks all around the world are reluctant to let the market do its work, and raise interest rates or follow a managed ('dirty') float. Two reasons may explain the reluctance to rely on the market:

(a) The fear that depreciation due to the given inflation differential could seriously hurt the still vulnerable domestic banking and non-banking sector.

(b) The concern that depreciation could lead to higher inflation and thereby damage the monetary authorities' reputation.

With these typical original-sin problems, the fear is that depreciation may trigger a downturn in investors' confidence and result in even sharper reversals in net capital inflows.

The commitment problem is closely linked to the institutional settings of the financial sector in crisis countries. When capital account restrictions are lifted, the quality of supervision and monitoring of the financial sector, as well as the degree of international integration of the banking industry, plays a role in increasing or reducing financial fragility. Empirical findings, which will be presented later, suggest that the financial and capital markets of the EU and its East European accession countries are integrated and that a convergence of nominal interest rates is taking place. Financial sectors will, however, have to manage the transition towards the adoption of the Euro – a process which will require an exchange rate strategy of monetary stability. Fragility alone does not mean that a crisis will necessarily occur, but explains the importance of the exchange rate for macroeconomic stability.

The relevance of financial systems for stability and growth

The preeminent importance of the financial sector for stability and growth lies in the fact that, unlike the agricultural sector, for example, a crisis within the financial sector can lead to a general decline in production and output. The infliction of the macroeconomic level rather than adjustments of relative prices between industries and sectors within the economy causes the particular importance of banking and finance for both stability and growth. The financial sector can principally described as the market place for stocks of wealth with an asymmetric relationship between borrowers and creditors. A crisis that goes with the devaluation of assets would reciprocally lead to a revaluation of debt, the so-called 'debt deflation' (Fisher 1933). The rate of interest for this debt service as the flow category generated by the stock of debts will rise and the 'real' economy will have to earn this service by surplus production.

The way in which the financial sector can contribute to macroeconomic stability is in the first place not to undergo a crisis – i.e. to be robust. This 'soundness' of banking and finance is best regarded as the institutional infrastructure in which markets function. Such an institutional infrastructure will go beyond the legal framework – contracts, bankruptcy and competition law – and includes a regulatory framework of financial markets as pertains in other key industries such as telecommunication, gas, water, and energy. These key industries are regulated by cost structures that can lead to the emergence of monopolies financial services; the financial services should be regulated because 'macroeconomic stability is an intermediate public good whose provision cannot be contracted out to the private sector' (Buiter *et al.* 1997, p. 20). Although the theory of public goods has been shattered since Coase showed that even lighthouses could be run efficiently by private firms, a closer look at the anatomy of financial crises will show the need for state activity.

Although the reasons for financial crises can be manifold, four main causes can be located within the domestic economy. First of all, an increase in interest rates initiated by the central bank, for whatever good reasons, can lead to *credit rationing*, in which case some investment projects will not be financed by banks although they would be profitable under the conditions of higher interest rates. According to Stiglitz and Weiss (1981), in such a situation the borrowers with high-risk projects will succeed in obtaining loans and the banking sector as a whole will reduce its volume of lending in order to reduce the level of risk. Based on the assumption of asymmetric information between borrowers and lenders (here, banks) a use in interest rates will increase financial instability through rising adverse selection. The rate of interest is not operating as market-clearing price and in anticipation of the theory of a financial crash it is even possible that a slight increase in interest may lead to a decline in the volume of lending and subsequently of investment and the level of aggregate economic activity. Declining incomes would then cause a cumulative process towards a fully fledged economic crisis.

It has to be added that the rise of interest rates might not be home-made, but initiated by the rise of interest rates in one of the key currencies or globally rising interest rates, which cannot be buffered by an exchange rate policy. The exchange rate itself can be the reason for the start of a financial crisis, because international capital movements can force a devaluation of the exchange rate to such a degree that it cannot be counterbalanced by improved competitiveness of exports. To show this possibility of external shocks, Box 3.1 separates the external and internal causes of financial crises. Although Box 3.1 does not explicitly show it, it should be mentioned that an exchange rate revaluation can also cause external destabilization. In that case the increasing overvaluation of the exchange rate will drive the balance of trade into deficit and increase foreign indebtedness.

The second reason for financial instability is described as a 'deterioration in the bank's balance sheets'. This can be caused directly by an increase in the rate of interest as this process devalues 'real' assets such as the net value of a firm against nominal assets such as bonds. Usually a deterioration in the balance sheet begins with unexpected defaults of loans for enterprises with insufficient collateral to cover their losses. A particular form of the same principle is a decline in the stock market, which would decrease the value of collateral, as the net market value of firms would decrease. This may be mentioned as a third reason for financial crises, as the dynamics of a stock market crash can cause defaults of banks and may affect the banking sector as a whole.

The fourth and most fundamental reason for a financial sector crisis is an increase in uncertainty, which refers back to the general unpredictability of the transformation process, described in Chapter 2. An increase in uncertainty would boost the desire to hold liquidity and subsequently increase the price for giving up liquidity. The rise of liquidity preference would therefore lead to an increase in interest rates and create the consequences outlined above. The degree of uncertainty can then grow to such an extent that no interest rate may be able to attract individuals to hold liquidity and domestic money at all. Subsequently there is capital flight abroad and into 'real' assets such as land due to the uncertainty normally be associated with political instability.

Whether one or all of these reasons are responsible for the financial crises, the sequence will always be initiated by increasing adverse selection and increasing moral-hazard behaviour. This will not be a change of individual behaviour as such, but an adjustment of the behaviour assumed in normal conditions to that in a serious situation caused by the higher degree of instability within the financial sector. Rising lack of transparency alone will lead a higher demand for loans, which are never intended to be paid back. It is not people, who begin to panic, but that a change of circumstances due to the above reasons has had consequences for the economy as a whole.

The sequence of such behaviour of the economy would begin with a crisis within the banking sector. If this is a serious crisis the assumption would be that it was not possible to contain it within the national financial system and it would spread over the border and there would be a change in the choice of currency by some international asset portfolios. This reaction, which is sometimes executed even without someone pressing a button on a PC but by a computer programme alone, would increase the supply of domestic currency and subsequently cause it to be devalued. This devaluation would push up import prices and lead to an inflationary situation for the affected economy. The fourth step in the sequence would be the crisis in the balance of payments. In order to stop the capital flight and to defend the domestic currency the central bank would have to raise interest rates astronomically. This in turn would accelerate the domestic banking crisis and might even lead to its collapse. The balance of payments crisis might accompany imposition of capital controls, which would feed an devaluation expectations further.

The fifth step would consist in falling production, leading to the sixth step of falling real income or rising unemployment. The sixth step would be the more painful the higher the proportion of foreign debt in domestic enterprises, as the devaluation of the domestic currency will increase the value of that debt and cause bankruptcies.

The worst-case scenario would be a seventh step of a 'global devaluation race', as experienced in the 1930s.

Consolidation of financial crises usually involves some kind of bailout, either externally by international organizations such as the IMF or the World Bank, or internally by the state. In reality, we normally find a combination of both types of consolidation, ending up with an increase of foreign debt and state debt. The problem with this type of consolidation is that some economies may be so poor that they find themselves caught within a debt trap in the aftermath of a financial crisis, because the burden of the debt service is too high to be matched by capital inflows – foreign investment and export surpluses. The general fallacy of consolidation by bailout and liquidation is that incentives are set to borrow and lend irresponsibly.

In view of this anatomy of financial crises, government intervention is unlikely to succeed within the course of the crisis itself, in particular as cumulative dynamics have to be assumed, which are not reflected in Box 3.3.

Box 3.3 Anatomy of a financial sector crisis

1. Reasons
- External:
  - exchange rate devaluation
  - globally rising interest rates
- Internal:
  - increasing rates of interest
  - deterioration of bank's balance sheet
  - stock market declines
  - increasing uncertainty

2. Sequence
  (1) Initial factors
   - increasing adverse selection
   - increasing moral-hazard behaviour
  (2) Banking crisis
  (3) Capital flight, currency devaluation, inflation
  (4) Balance of payments crisis
  (5) Decreasing production
  (6) Decreasing income
  (7) Deflation

3. Consolidation
- External: 'bailout', increase in foreign debt
- Internal: liquidation, 'bailout', increase in government debt

---

Priority therefore has to be given to setting the rules of the game by the state, a case of classical German-type *Ordnungspolitik* (see Hölscher 1998). A government strategy to obtain financial sector stability would consist of two main components: setting of generally binding *standards* and tough *supervision* of the financial sector. However, there are at least two features that make this approach to financial markets more difficult than in goods markets. Financial markets are *global markets* and standards for trafficking in finance ought to reflect this nature by being globally applicable, although there is not a global institution in place to supervise such global rules. Secondly financial markets have proved to be extremely innovative in their products, and legislation as well as supervision can easily end up in a position of being always one step too late to maintain control of the situation.

Even if the possibility of setting standards is assumed, the harder part is then maintaining those standards (see Goodhart 1997). Normal moral-hazard behaviour is particularly relevant within the financial system, because a system of incentives and sanctions has to reflect that the state itself is a major player in the system, partly due to deposit insurance but principally through the institution of the central bank. Independent auditing is one way of approaching the problem, but still leaves the details of who would be in charge for hiring, firing and paying the auditor unresolved. Since the realization of some kind of *Ordnungspolitik* has proved to be difficult for financial sectors, the question remains as to what type of regulatory policies can be applied.

Three types of regulatory policies can be distinguished for the financial sector. The first and most obvious is *monetary policy* itself, which means in the extreme case of a collapsing financial sector caused by bank runs that the central bank acts as LOLR in order to prevent asset deflation like that experienced in the 1930s. Such a policy can only be an exceptional response, however, as it has *per se* destabilizing inflationary effects.

Secondly, the formal *regulation* of the financial sector itself is a traditional but effective approach to promoting stability. Banking activities can subject to licensing as well as permanent monitoring. Normally market entry is not free, nor is market exit. Rules for certain ratios within the balance sheet as well as market behaviour could be the basis for the (temporary) closure of institutions. Competition policy would be part of this regulation policy.

Finally the protection against foreign factors creating domestic financial crises would require some auditing of exposure against foreign exchange risk (see Buch and Heinrich 1998, p. 24), although the balance of payments position of a country can really only be influenced by macroeconomic stability.

The case of transition economies is even more challenging, as here not only stability but growth is required. Dynamic growth rates are the prime aim of economic transition in order to catch up with western countries. The relevant question for a sound financial sector is thus not only how to support monetary stability, but how the financial sector can promote growth.

If the basic decision to invest is taken as the choice of demand for credit to finance an investment project, or not to invest in it, the general condition for investment would be that profit expectations exceed the cost of investment finance – i.e. the rate of interest. For the sake of simplicity, profit expectations of the entrepreneurial sector are assumed as exogenous. Furthermore the interest rate policy of the central bank is assumed to be instrumental for matching the inflation target of macroeconomic stability and cannot be used for the encouragement of investment by a low interest rate policy during transition. Now the relationship between growth and the financial sector in the transition to fully fledged market economies is isolated, and the contribution of the financial sector to growth can only be to supply the lowest possible lending rates. As the restrictive assumption of this approach is the impossibility of a low interest policy of the central bank, lower lending rates can be achieved only by a decreasing spread of deposit and lending rates within the financial sector. The soundness of the financial sector would be indicated by narrow spreads.

Although high interest rate spreads can contribute to the stability of the financial sector itself by allowing it to build up (hidden) reserves or to write off bad assets, this does not change the main line of the argument promoted here. In the dynamic context of system transformation the process of declining spreads would indicate success in cleaning up the banks' portfolios. From an equilibrium analysis point of view this process would enter some type of steady state, when world market spreads were achieved. This also implies that such banks would then be able to compete with foreign financial institutions.

From a Schumpeterian point of view, quasi-rents in the banking sector could be fruitful to write off bad debts and would diminish in the process of domestic competition over time. The absence of those quasi-rents would indicate a maturity to enter international competition. The institutional dimension of this gradual decline in spreads would allow banks to grow into their role as the ephor (controller) of the exchange economy (Schumpeter 1911) to carry out their overseeing functions of control and screening.

The strategy of '*semi*-liberalization'

Taking up the basic question of this chapter – how the banking sector can contribute to macroeconomic stability during transition – on the basis of the above country cases we argue in favour of a careful rehabilitation of the financial sector with foreign participation. This suggests a policy option that lies between the two radical solutions of 'free entry' and full rehabilitation. Table 3.1 summarizes the different policy options for the restructuring of the banking system and demonstrates the crucial link between a liberalization strategy and the bad debt solution.

A flow solution of the bad debt problem seems not to be feasible without a far-reaching liberalization. CEE banks with bad assets are less competitive than new or foreign institutions, because they can not offer such competitive rates. The rebuilding of the bad debts must have an obligatory character; it does not allow for new competitors. The direct investment facilities provided by a liberalized capital market also offer arbitrage

Table 3.1   Liberalization and the bad debt solution

Solution	Level of liberalization			
Bad debt solution	*Rehabilitation*	*Joint ventures (JVs) with banks*	*Capital market liberalization*	*Free entry*
State solution	Domestic German type	German type	(Domestic) Anglo-Saxon type	Anglo-Saxon type; failures of domestic banks likely
Flow solution	Domestic German type	German type	Feasibility doubtful Danger of banking crises	Not feasible

opportunities and undermine the feature of intertemporal smoothing through variations in banks' (hidden) reserves.

A flow solution of the bad asset problem calls for a German type of financial system, with the additional opportunity to exploit favourable macroeconomic constellations. Economic growth is necessary to write off the bad debts. In the light of the absence of any banking history the typical arguments in favour of a full rehabilitation strategy, which builds on local knowledge and an existing link between the banking and productive sectors, look quite weak. Instead, JVs in the banking sector may lead to a contribution of foreign capital and management experience within this process, but foreign investors will contribute only if profit expectations are really high.

Within an Anglo-Saxon system of liberalized capital markets a flow solution of the bad asset problem is not feasible. Even if the domestic capital market takes over the role of funding for investment and the banks' role is restricted to offering payment facilities, a banking crisis is very likely to occur. Sooner or later the bad debts end up on the state's balance sheet. Free entry for foreign banks and foreign competition will have an immediate effect. Most importantly, a liberalization of the capital market is already a prerequisite for the development of the financial system, because banks lose the ability to build up (hidden) reserves in order to buffer intertemporal fluctuations of the business cycle.

So far the CEE countries have seen only one outright successful case of bank restructuring (see Chapter 9). This 'Hungarian model' supported macroeconomic stability and growth while securing efficient allocation of investments and savings through domestic competition. On the other hand, the Czech Republic went through a fully fledged financial crisis, which led to a serious setback in the Czech transition progress as a whole. The crucial point is the interrelationship between current account and financial sector improvements. A lesson from the world economic crisis of the 1930s is that one would normally expect the central bank to fight internal banking crises by opening up the discount window and creating liquidity. This is not an option for the transition countries under review.[1] The bank run took place in hard currency, and domestic interest rates could not prevent capital flight into the D-Mark and the US dollar. In this sense, CEE banking sectors will be vulnerable to speculative currency attacks for a long time. In a world of global currency competition a strategy of *semi*-liberalization may lead to integration instead of simply being taken over.

The evolution of financial institutions

Transition countries had not only to build up financial sectors from scratch, but also had to deal with the inherited balance sheets of the socialist monobank system (see Chapter 2). Savings were accumulated in the past, not because deposit interest rates could be realized, but due to a lack of spending options. These deposits were forced savings, which did not follow any market calculus. On the other side of the balance sheet there were the administered loans given to SOEs.

The state monobank system was rotten to its core and early hopes that these problems would go away with high inflation, leading to a devaluation of the purchasing power of consumers, overlooked the stock problem referred to as 'bad loans' or 'bad asset' problems. 'Bad loans' are dubious assets, which need to be written off. They are classified as non-performing loans in the bank's balance sheet and harm the profitability and competitiveness of the financial institution. Even in 2002 all transition

Table 3.2 Non-performing loans as a percentage of total loan portfolios, 2002

Country	(%)
Czech Republic	13.8
Hungary	3.4
Poland	17.8
Slovakia	21.9
Slovenia	5.4

Source: National Bank of Poland.

countries except Hungary and Slovenia were displaying double-digit percentages of 'bad loans' in their portfolios (Table 3.2).

If this inherited debt problem is not resolved, the debt burden grows inexorably through accumulating interest obligations. These are the free ways of resolving the 'bad asset' problem:

- **Write off**
  This requires building up retained earnings through operating profits of the bank, which can be supported by tax allowances.
- **Debt–equity swap**
  'Bad loans' are replaced by government bonds and transferred into a specialist agency. This means that the taxpayer has to bear the inherited debts.
- **Auction**
  'Bad assets' are sold to the public by auction for a fraction of their book value. This is only a partial solution, which leaves the institution with a residue of 'bad loans' in the balance sheet.
- **Liquidation**
  The enterprise is closed down and the bank goes bankrupt.
- **Enterprise restructuring**
  'Bad loans' are turned into good loans by restructuring debtors. This requires time and probably fresh investment.

The low proportion of bad loans in Slovenia and Hungary can be attributed to successful restructuring of the banking sector in general and the approach towards the 'bad asset' problem in particular.

Not much progress has been reported in the field of financial sector structures and developments. The CEE accession countries started from scratch with a monobank system and no capital markets at all. This legacy is still prevailing in the form of low levels of liquidity and financial intermediation. For example, stock market capitalization has not reached even 20 per cent of what can be found in the Euro area, the ratio of banking assets as a percentage of GDP is about one-third of Euroland levels, and domestic credit is a third of that in Euroland (see Table 3.3).

Before summarizing our conclusions from Table 3.3, some country-specific differences should be noted. Romania and Bulgaria are clearly lagging behind the other accession countries and even within the more advanced group of transition countries there are major outliers, such as the banking sector of the Czech Republic. With regard to stock market capitalization, Slovenia displays the highest ratio. While mentioning the differences among the transition countries, one should also be aware

Table 3.3 Financial sectors in the CEE accession countries, 2002

Country	Banking assets (% of GDP)	Domestic credit (% of GDP)	Stock market capitalization (% of GDP)
Bulgaria	44	21	4
Czech Republic	126	61	16
Estonia	72	43	27
Hungary	61	42	19
Latvia	77	25	9
Lithuania	32	18	10
Poland	66	39	14
Romania	30	13	3
Slovakia	96	67	19
Slovenia	79	56	30
All	68	39	15
Euro area	265	135	72
Cyprus	249	137	69
Malta	224	147	37

Source: ECB (2002).

of major differences among the financial sectors within the European Union. Stock market capitalization in the United Kingdom, for example, is about five times what it is in Germany. There are also prevailing differences in financial intermediation between Greece, Portugal, and the rest of the European Union. Here the benchmark would ideally consist between the two other newcomers to the union (Cyprus and Malta) and the transition countries. Table 3.3 shows that these countries are almost at the average EU level as far as institutional financial depth is concerned, which makes the transition countries of special interest.

Two explanations for the position of transition economics are feasible. First these countries could still be suffering from the legacies of the past in that there is still a high level of general uncertainty. This would result into a more cash-oriented society reflected in a low financial sector development at the institutional level. Secondly, the newly emerging financial sectors may have taken advantage of the rapid increase in financial innovation in the 1990s. This led to a huge proportion of off-balance sheet transactions, as reflected in ratios within Table 3.3. However, both hypothetical explanations lack clear empirical evidence.

The huge *prima facie* gap in financial intermediation between central and western Europe could lead to the hypothesis that there is still a long way to go before financial integration is complete. It will be interesting to see what the data show, but one qualitative observation should be included in this institutional background. The banking sector seems to have been successfully stabilized, although this has implied an almost complete takeover by West European banks – i.e. full institutional integration. Also, as the Czech banking and balance of payment crisis has shown, the transition countries can easily become subject to speculative attacks again. In general, the pre-accession scenario of financial sector development looked fairly different from the general EU situation and CEE financial sectors must still to be considered as being fragile.

Note

1. Experience has shown that this is not even an option for an economy like Russia.

References and further reading

Begg, D. (1996) 'Monetary policy in Central and Eastern Europe: lessons after half a decade of transition', IMF Working Paper WP/96/108.

Borish, M. S., W. Ding and M. Noel (1997) 'A review of bank performance in Central Europe', *Communist Economies & Economic Transformation* 9(3).

Buch, C. M. (1997) 'Opening up for Foreign Banks – why Central and Eastern Europe can benefit', *Economics of Transition* 5 (2).

Buch, C. and R. P. Heinrich (1998) 'Banking and balance of payments crises – on possible causes of the twin crises', The Kiel Institute of World Economics, Kiel Working Paper 848.

Buiter, W., R. Lago and Stern N. (1997) Promoting an Effective Market Economy in a Changing World,' CEPR Discussion Paper No. 1468, London.

Eichengreen, B. and Hausmann (1999) *Exchange Rates and Financial Fragility*, NBER Working Paper No. W7418, Cambridge, MA.

European Bank for Reconstruction and Development (EBRD) (1997) *Transition Report*, London.

European Central Bank (2002) 'The Eurosystem's dialogue with EU accession countries', *Monthly Bulletin*, July.

Fisher, I. (1933) 'The debt–deflation theory of great depressions', *Econometrica* 1, pp. 337–357.

Gabrisch, H. and R. Pohl (eds) (1999) *EU Enlargement and its Macroeconomic Effects in Eastern Europe* (London and New York: Macmillan and St Martin's Press).

Goodhart, C. A. E. (1997) 'Setting standards is just the first step: maintaining them is the harder part', paper presented at the University of Birmingham, mimeo.

Herten, S. and J. Hölscher (2001) 'Capital and credit based development – lessons from the experience of industrial countries for transition economies in Central East Europe', in W. Buiter, S. F. Frowen and F. McHugh (eds), *Financial Competition, Risk and Accountability* (London and New York: Macmillan and St Martin's Press).

Hölscher, J. (1998) 'Zur Formierung marktwirtschaflicher Ordnungen in Zentralosteuropa', *Applied Economics Quarterly, Konjunkturpolitik* 1998/4.

Hölscher, J. with M. Jarmuzek (2005) Over- or undervalued Euroland entry?', *Post-Communist Economies* 17, pp. 235–50.

Kaser, M. (1990) 'The technology of decontrol: some macroeconomic issues,' *Economic Journal*, 100 (401), pp. 596–615.

Kregel, J. (1996) 'Transformational development, the problem of inflation and financial structure', in J. Hölscher, A. Jacobsen, H. Tomann, and H. Weisfeld (eds), *Conditions of Economic Development in Central and Eastern Europe, Vol. 5: Economic Policy and Development Strategies in Central and Eastern Europe* (Marburg: Metropolis).

McKinnon, R. I. and H. W. Pill (1997) 'Credible economic liberalization and overborrowing', *American Economic Review*, Papers and Proceedings, 87(2), pp. 189–93.

Melo, M. de and C. Denizer (1997) 'Monetary policy during transition – an overview', World Bank, Policy Research Working Paper 1706.

Mishkin, F. S. (1997) 'International capital movements, financial volatility and financial instability', paper presented to the annual meeting of the 'Verein für Socialpolitik', Bern, mimeo.

National Bank of Hungary (1997) *Annual Report 1996, Monthly Report 9/1997* (Budapest).

OECD (ed.) (1997) 'The new banking landscape in Central and Eastern Europe', *OECD Proceedings* (Paris: OECD).

Schumpeter, J. A. (1911) *Theorie der wirtschaftlichen Entwicklung* (Berlin: Duncker & Humblot).

Stephan, J. (1999) *Economic Transition in Hungary and East Germany* (London and New York: Macmillan and St Martin's Press).

Stern, N. and J. Stiglitz (1997) 'A framework for a development strategy in a market economy: objectives, scope, institutions and instruments', Working Paper 20 (London: EBRD).

Stiglitz, J. E. and A. Weiss (1981) 'Credit rationing in markets with imperfect information', *American Economic Review*, 73, pp. 912–27.

Tomann, H. (1997) 'Options for resolving the "bad asset problem" ', in S. Frowen and J. Hölscher (eds), The *German Currency Union of 1990 – A Critical Assessment* (London and New York: Macmillan and St Martin's Press).

Winkler, A. (1996) 'Macroeconomic stabilisation in transition economies: the relevance of financial system development', Discussion Papers in German Studies IGS96/6 (University of Birmingham).

4
Privatization and Competition

Chapter 4 addresses the relationship between ownership transformation and the establishment of competition. Competition is the driving force of an innovative market economy with private ownership. But privatization – the core of ownership transformation – is a necessary policy to generate a competitive private sector, but it is far from being sufficient. We discuss the problem of the 'soft' budget constraint, which prevails in CPEs with state-owned firms and which is a stubborn attendant of transition, when ownership transformation is conducted in a non-competitive way and a non-competitive environment. A taxonomy of privatization presents the various ways in which ownership transformation has been pursued. Finally the difficulties in creating a competitive environment are illustrated with an analysis of anti-trust policy in transition countries.

From state to private ownership

The emerging private sector

The expansion of the private sector started from different levels in individual countries. Agriculture was overwhelmingly private in Poland, also handicrafts. The state-owned sector was the largest in the GDR, Czechoslovakia, and Russia. Where a small private sector existed, was it under the rigid control of the government in terms of aggregate production plans, price settings and provisions for production inputs. A cooperative sector existed in all countries, mainly in trade, handicrafts, and other services. Although the state was not the owner, cooperatives were under strict government control. While the private sector almost vanished in the 1960s and 1970s, it regained some strength in the 1980s, for it acted as a compensation for the failures of central planning. There emerged not only a remarkable shadow economy, but some legal provisions supported an official private sector. In Poland, for example, foreigners of Polish origin could establish small firms in the 1970s and 1980s. The ownership picture of the socialist Yugoslavia was completely different. 'Socially owned' companies and 'workers' self governance' made the country quite distinct from the Soviet type of universal state ownership.

After 1990, the rapid expansion of the private sector stemmed from two sources: *de novo* companies established by private persons and foreign investors, and privatization of SOEs. Although one can dispute the meaning and measurement of a private sector (see Box 4.1), Figure 4.1 illustrates the impressive rise of the private sector in terms of GDP in a decade.

Box 4.1   What is a private sector?

Some economists insist that only economic activities that are fully controlled by private entrepreneurs are qualified to form a 'private' sector. Others insist that all the economic activities that are not fully controlled by the government are so qualified. It is difficult to provide an unambiguous measure for public–private activities. For China, no comparable data are available. Some estimates are based on the 'individual economy', which excludes collective firms run by private persons, foreign-invested companies, small unincorporated businesses, individually invested corporatized enterprises, and partnerships. The private sector in China is thus larger than is reported. There is also a debate about the character of Chinese Township and Village Enterprises (TVEs). TVEs can be established by local authorities and are not centrally controlled. Some economists define them as 'quasi-private', others as 'quasi-state-owned' companies.

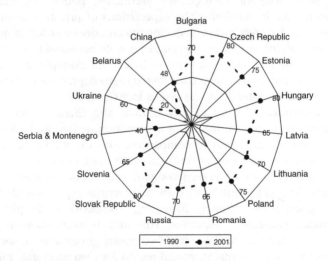

Figure 4.1   The private sector's share in GDP in per cent

Sources: EBRD, Transition Report, 2002 and 1997; for China (1975, 1998) various sources.

Institutional prerequisites for privatization: financial markets and competition

For our purposes 'private ownership' means the right to sell, which implies an institutional set-up in which such sales are possible. In the market-oriented paradigm private property is regarded not just as a physical asset but also a value category of the asset markets, which are ultimately dominated by the financial markets. As elaborated in Chapter 3, the institutional structure of financial markets was actually non-existent at the start of transition. It needs private and public initiatives to develop the norms and regulations to solve commitment problems over time. Foreign financial markets can give some assistance, but overwhelmingly for small countries (such the Baltic States) only the size of it will be of some relevance. Larger countries need domestic solutions, in particular in the first stage of transition, when the investment risk for international investors is still very high.

The lack of financial institutions has two major consequences for privatization: the first is that the *value* of state-owned assets can merely be evaluated as a market value as in a fully fledged market economy. The high financial risk in privatizing a company necessarily devalues the possible price of that asset. The second consequence is that the financial markets are not able to provide sufficient financial means for investment. Economic development depends almost completely on profits and private domestic savings. Macroeconomic policy has, then, a prominent role in stabilizing the expectations of private households, managers, and entrepreneurs. Reducing uncertainty by ensuring output and price stability enhances the value of private households' savings in banks and the inclination of firms to invest. An example of how the macroeconomic environment contributed to the depreciation of savings is provided in Chapter 9, for the case of East Germany.

The institutional set-up of privatization and financial markets is closely related to the institution of competition. Financial markets are able to value an asset only in comparison with the market success of other assets. The inclusion of competition in our considerations opens the perspective to a specific dichotomy: the economic rationale for privatization lies, on the one hand, with the potential improvement of corporate governance through increasing competition. Simply put, *privatization establishes competition.* The implicit assumption in such reasoning is that the poor quality of corporate governance in socialist countries is a fundamental structural reason for their economic misfortune. This assumption suggests that the economic crisis at the end of the socialist era can in part be explained by 'overinvestment' in unprofitable projects due to a lack of a competitive environment. This disregard of profit as investment criterion resulted from a systematic absence of alternative assets and led to non-market governance mechanisms, which in one form or another continued throughout the transformation period. The literature on planned economies and economies in transition applies the concept of *'soft' budget constraints* (SBC) in describing this basic weakness of the command economy (see Box 4.2).

The SBC syndrome, on the other hand, is not necessarily linked with the ownership issue, but rather with the *lack of competition*, which may emerge also in market economies. Seen from this perspective, privatization is only a necessary but not a sufficient means to establish new efficient decision-making procedures – an argument impressively confirmed by transitional China without any privatization. A *competitive environment* is the institutional prerequisite in market economies, if a public company is successfully to privatize. Competition guarantees transparency, which in turn prevents corruption. Potential investors and banks or the capital market are able to value the firm's assets, for they know the product market of the firm and its competitors. The value of its assets is always a relative

---

Box 4.2 The 'soft' budget constraint syndrome

The Hungarian economist Janos Kornai invented the term SBC in the 1980s for the analysis of the specific causes of the inefficiency of socialist economies, rooted in the paternalistic relation between the state and its SOEs. The modern SBC syndrome is a metaphor describing a situation in which the government or a bank bails out a company (private or state-owned) in the case of financial problems (see Kornai, Maskin and Roland 2003). With SBC, a privatized firm has a moral-hazard problem: the managers have more information about the projects they intend to propose for financing than the government or their bank. They know that a poor project may be bailed out. Hence, they submit good as well as poor projects, and by financing a certain share of poor projects, the conditions for the sector of *de novo* private firms deteriorate. A bailout may happen in various ways. A state bailout is often linked with tax arrears. The EBRD estimated (EBRD 2002) that, on average, one-quarter of all firms in the eight new EU member countries had tax arrears in 1998, with the highest shares (almost 40 per cent) in the Czech Republic and Slovakia. Another form is to withhold the payment of bills to state-owned utility providers. This was a phenomenon met especially in Russia, where tax arrears were lower than in the Czech and Slovak Republics. Finally, when the debt of a company, even a privatized one, against the banking sector is on the rise, despite falling profitability, then it can be seen as evidence for a SBC even in a market economy (Schaffer 1998). Konings and Vandenbussche (2004) made an econometric analysis of all the large and medium-sized firms (mostly privatized firms) in Bulgaria. They found that 27 per cent of them were subject to SBC in the post-socialist era. The incidence of a 'soft' budget through loans to large and medium-sized firms was much more prevalent in Bulgaria than in, for example, Belgium (9.5 per cent), a West European country similar in size.

price, measured in terms of the success of its competitors. The environment of transition economies is completely different: the state-owned firm, above all the large ones in the capital-intensive industries, is a monopoly: a relative asset price cannot be established. What is more, privatization of a monopoly simply initially establishes a private monopoly, which is in no way superior in terms of corporate governance and efficiency. A non-transparent privatization process may also contribute to excessive corruption. Therefore, we follow the dictum 'the more competition the better' as a specific challenge for transformation in creating a competitive environment for privatization and for privatized firms.[1]

A taxonomy of privatization methods

'Insider' and 'outsider' privatization

We have now provided a guide for the assessment of privatization methods that follows. The checklist for this guide includes the ability of privatization methods to mobilize savings, to establish competitive structures, to enhance the creation of financial markets, and to prevent corruption.

Initially, the nascent private sector earned an income from small privatization and restitution. Small privatization included handicrafts, wholesale and retail trade, flats, services (transport), and even public toilets. To this we may add the restitution of earlier nationalized property, mostly also smaller firms. All this helped in job creation with little capital. Our interest here is in the large privatization that included medium-sized and large SOEs. The restructuring and development of these companies under competition required significant finance, new technology, managerial know-how, and corporate control. Privatization policy in each country used a mixture of methods, and the establishment of the rule of competition did not always have primacy.

A classification of methods often met in the literature is the distinction between insider and outsider privatization. 'Insider privatization' means that managers and/or employees take the assets of the firm. An inherent problem of insider privatization is the possible inferiority of insiders against outsiders that narrows the access of the company to capital, technology, and managerial knowledge. If insider-dominated firms do not overcome this internal behaviour barrier, they will be doomed to die. Insider privatization methods, regulated by legislation, are management or employee buy-outs (MEBO). Insider privatization also includes 'spontaneous privatization' that is a more or less illegal form of asset transfer. 'Outsider privatization' means that other domestic owners or foreign investors are the new owners. Typical new owners are foreign investors, domestic and foreign investment funds, and foreign consulting companies. Among outsider privatization in transition countries, the distribution of vouchers and direct sales (via auctions or tenders) dominated. Management buy-outs (MBO) and Employee buy-outs (EBO) were the primary privatization method in twelve of the twenty-seven countries in Table 4.1, followed by voucher privatization (nine) and direct

Table 4.1 Leading methods of privatization

	Method of privatization	
Country	**Primary**	**Secondary**
Czech Republic	Voucher	Direct sale
Hungary	Direct sale	MEBO
East Germany	Direct sale	MEBO
Estonia	Direct sale	Voucher
Slovakia	Direct sale	Voucher
Lithuania	Voucher	Direct sale
Poland	Direct sale	MEBO
Albania	MEBO	Voucher
Bulgaria	Direct sale	Voucher
Latvia	MEBO	Voucher
Russia[a]	Voucher	Direct sale
Armenia	Voucher	MEBO
Georgia	Voucher	Direct sale
Romania	MEBO	Voucher
Slovenia	MEBO	Voucher
Kazakhstan	Voucher	MEBO
Ukraine	MEBO	Direct sale
Croatia	MEBO	Voucher
Macedonia, FRY	MEBO	Direct sale
Kyrgyz Republic	Voucher	MEBO
Azerbaijan	MEBO	Voucher
Moldova	Voucher	Direct sale
Tajikistan	Direct sale	Voucher
Uzbekistan	MEBO	Direct sale
Bosnia & Herzegovina	Voucher	Direct sale
Serbia & Montenegro	Direct sale[b]	n.a.
Turkmenistan	MEBO	Direct sale
Belarus	MEBO	Voucher

Notes:
[a] Dominantly manufacturing.
[b] Since 1991.
n.a.: Not available.
FRY: Former Republic of Yugoslavia.

Source: EBRD (1999, 2002).

sales (seven). Direct sales dominated in EU candidate and accession countries, while MEBOs were found mostly in less advanced transition countries in the 1990s. Estrin and Angelucci (2003) found that the share of insider-owned firms decreased over time, demonstrating that firms changed ownership by resale, sometimes called 'second privatization'.

Buy-outs

In case of MEBO privatizations, medium and smaller enterprises which could not attract foreign capital and were endangered by liquidation were sold. The main problem with MEBOs is that the 'insiders' – the managers or the employees – can offer only a minor amount of capital for development. MEBOs face more competition than large privatized companies on their product markets and have a very restricted access to information about credit, new technologies, and other resources. The ownership structure is dispersed in the case of EBOs, establishing a severe corporate governance problem; it makes the credit problem worse. Insider privatized firms tend to prefer *defensive restructuring strategies,* which include cuts in wages and social provisions, the liquidation of unprofitable products, the shedding of excess labour, and the sale or leasing out of excess equipment. It is a matter of long-run survival that this strategy changes after a certain time in favour of the introduction of new products and services, quality-raising innovation, changes in the management, etc. (active or 'deep' restructuring). Insider firms rely on the accumulated social and institutional capital of the firm, not only in relations between managers and workers, but also in relation to supplier and customers. Defensive restructuring can turn into deep restructuring after a period of consolidation, which in turn is a prerequisite for attracting outside investors. How this can happen demonstrates the example of the large Slovenian company 'Gorenje' (see Box 4.3).

Box 4.3   'Insider' privatization: the case of Gorenje (Slovenia)

Gorenje is a company producing household appliances. The Gorenje group traditionally held a strong presence in west European markets before the break-up of the former Yugoslavia (60 per cent of its output went to western Europe). With a staff of about 10,000 the group was among the largest enterprises in Yugoslavia. In Yugoslavia, an enterprise had the legal status of 'socially owned capital' – the typical circumscription of the Yugoslav system for nobody's ownership with a strategic position of the workers' council and with cheap finance provided by government-influenced banks.

Continued

Box 4.3 Continued

Slovenia started gradual ownership transformation in 1992. The population received vouchers to be changed into shares of investment funds or companies to be privatized. Investment funds could be established by banks and consulting agencies. The decision on privatisation was transferred to the workers' council of each company. Companies could freely decide among six methods of privatization: (1) sale of shares to the employees, (2) free distribution of shares among employees, (3) sale of shares by public offering and tenders (= voucher), (4) liquidation of the company, (5) transformation by the issue of new shares, and (6) transfers of shares to the state-owned development funds. However, in each case, 40 per cent of all shares were to be transferred to three state funds (pension funds, compensation funds, and development funds). The sale to foreign owners was allowed, but rarely took place. The Gorenje workers' council voted for a mixed procedure in 1994. 20 per cent of shares were internally distributed, 25 per cent were sold to employees, 15 per cent went for public sale to investment funds and other voucher holders (the remaining 40 per cent went to the public funds). The internal distribution compensated for an earlier nominal wage payment cut of 20 per cent. Employees with a higher wage (among the management) received more shares than workers with low wages. The distribution of shares was completed in 1996, however, the transformation into a joint stock company occurred only in 1998. Today, the two major shareholders are state-owned ones – the pension funds and the compensation funds (the latter deals with restitution matters in Slovenia). Government influence is even larger: the state-owned development fund and some investment funds (established and partly owned by still state-owned banks) hold some shares. In general, the government can directly or indirectly influence about 45 per cent of ownership. The shares are tradable on the Ljubljana Stock Exchange.

Until 1998, a provisional supervisory board, elected by the workers' council, controlled the board of managers. Since then, the corporate governance system has been a two-tier one, following the German example: the supervisory board, elected by the shareholders, consists of ten members, of which five are elected by the annual assembly of shareholders; five are delegated by the workers' council. With regard to the fact that the employees of Gorenje hold a significant part of the shares, the supervisory board is clearly insider-dominated, the remainder of the shares are controlled by public organizations. The management board consists of five members, of which the workers' council delegates one. The strong insider orientation was responsible for the fact that the personal composition of the management board did not change between 1990 and 1998. In 2003, among the management board, two were outsiders.

The break-up of Yugoslavia entailed the loss of the important markets of Serbia and, Croatia. Further, the only major change in the environment was the imposition of 'hard' budget constraints on the firm. The practice of easy credit stopped when transition started, and Gorenje started to go into the red. The first response of the company to the new situation was defensive restructuring: the management, the workers' council and the trade unions agreed a nominal

Continued

Box 4.3   Continued

cut of wage cut to be compensated by future privatization. The staff shrank to some 5,000 by 1992, two companies left the group, and Gorenje concentrated on its core business – household appliances. The slow privatization of Gorenje preserved the social and institutional capital. Between 1992 and 1994, first signs of deep restructuring emerged: using the Europe-wide network relations strengthened innovation activities. The company went into the black once again in 1994. Because of preferential trade agreements between Slovenia and the other successor states, the former Yugoslav markets could be regained. Today, the company again employs a staff of 10,000. However, Slovenia's access to the European Union poses new challenges. The favourable trade agreements with the other successor states have to be replaced because of the higher EU custom tariffs. New adjustment efforts will be necessary, including the acquisition of foreign investors.

Voucher or mass privatization

Vouchers were distributed among the population at a very low nominal price, and could be changed into shares when SOEs were privatized. The political rationale behind mass privatization schemes was their high speed, the popular support, and the possibly low potential for corruption. Some transactions costs related to corruption might be low compared with other privatization methods (mainly direct sales), because the size of mass privatization required clearly specified rules and procedures, available for everybody, which reduced administrative discretion to firms going through the auction process. Voucher schemes also promised an equal distribution of state property, which in socialist ideology was interpreted as 'peoples' property'. This method promised to compensate the population for the real income losses during corrective inflation. Therefore, political parties and governments could gain more popular support for the necessary reforms.

Although mass privatization was 'outsider' privatization, there were some relevant disadvantages compared to other outsider forms. Ownership transfer yielded no concentrated ownership. The management and the employees (the insiders) might gain *de facto* the dominant position against the dispersed owners. Voucher privatized companies had a corporate governance problem, because the many outsider owners had little information on the management. With general asymmetric information between them and the managers, the transaction costs for active restructuring the firm became high. Either job destruction might dominate (see Jurajda and Terrell 2000, for the Czech Republic) or a second privatization would be necessary through the resale of shares to strategic investors.

Some authors state that the establishment and involvement of investment funds and banks in voucher privatization had a beneficial impact on the development of capital markets (Bennet *et al.* 2003). Actually however, voucher privatized firms affected the stability of the emerging banking sector. The inherited debt of privatized companies from the socialist era became a burden on the banking sector and led to persistent refinancing (see the SBC syndrome, p. 63) of the privatized firms, at the same time as restricting the access of the nascent private sector to credit. The share of bad credits in the banks' portfolio increased, contributing to higher spreads between credit and deposit interest rates to the detriment of the small- and medium-scale private firms (SMEs). The burden became so high that the banking sector was threatened by increasing fragility ending in a financial crisis (as in the Czech Republic 1997, and in Russia 1998).

Direct sales

At first glance, the participation of foreign investors via direct sales seemed to offer the most effective opportunities to mobilize the necessary resources for restructuring and sustainable growth in the absence of domestic finance and domestic strategic investors. The speed of direct sales depended on the availability of foreign investors, and was not necessarily slower than voucher privatization. Where this availability was given and the institutional environment was stable, privatization could proceed at high speed, as in East Germany, where most SOEs were split up and sold to west German firms within a couple of years. The investors decided to take over a plant that could be made competitive in a relatively short time. The sale involved negotiations with a few potential investors via auctions and tenders (low transaction costs for gaining trust) who competed with their price offer, their investment plans, or with other comparative advantage. The new foreign owner provided some additional financing and opened the way to accessing the social and institutional capital of the mother company. The actual problem with direct sales was that the transaction costs of restructuring were shifted to the tax payer instead to the markets and/or increased public debt instead of private debt, as in Germany. Privatization via direct sales to foreign companies did not necessarily enhance competition. International automotive companies forced the Polish government to restrict temporarily the import of cars after the previously respective trade was liberalized, otherwise they would not have bought the domestic plant. In addition, sales to foreigners were unpopular in many countries (for example, in Poland), not at least for a level of proneness corruption higher than in voucher privatization.

Misconducted privatization

Spontaneous privatization typically took place in transition countries when directors of SOEs received control over state property in the absence of any privatization law. Spontaneous privatization was 'insider' privatization and was frequently encouraged by the reluctance of early reform governments to take any responsibility for the SOEs and were pressurized by various lobbies. In its worst form, spontaneous privatization took the form of asset-stripping by the management – a phenomenon that could be observed during 1991 and 1992 in Russia. Asset-stripping meant that the uncontrolled management sold the better parts of the firm to a 'straw man' firm.

Loans for shares. Transition countries generally offered the conversion of debt into shares. However, the bad reputation of this method resulted from its specific application in Russia in 1995, when the government was out of cash. It included strategic enterprises, which had not yet been privatized by vouchers. The initiative came from the banks, which proposed to loan funds to the cash-strapped government with repayment secured by the government's majority stake in companies in the oil, gas, and nickel industry. The shares were given to those who lent the most money to the government. This kind of ('outsider') privatization contributed much to the birth of the new class of super-rich individuals (the oligarchs) in Russian society, even when spontaneous privatization had come to an end.

Spontaneous privatization and the loans for shares privatization in Russia had the worst distributional consequences. As we have seen, it gave birth the oligarchs (see Chapter 9). Like voucher privatization, political and economic power tended to become closely interrelated. This kind of privatization also contributed to the spread of mistrust of private ownership and the state administration.

A review of anti-trust practices in EU accession countries[2]

The mode of privatization is an issue that touches on the sensitive relations between private ownership and competition. The 'Washington Consensus' favoured a quick privatization of state enterprises; some authors found even oligarchs to be the engine for growth and reforms, since they were the only feasible counterweight to a predatory and corrupt Russian bureaucracy, and they were willing to invest. Stiglitz (2000) argued that misconducted privatization, leading to market power, would hamper the development of competition. The Russian privatization provides ample evidence of the market power of oligarchs in the resources sector and in the automotive industry (Guriev and Rachinsky 2005). These were the sectors of the Russian economy where huge wealth could be accumulated in the absence of any regulation of competition, and by excluding foreign competition. The market and political power of the oligarchs made later competition laws ineffective in Russia, due to many exceptions and arbitrary handling by state authorities; Russia and also Ukraine fell significantly behind the leading EU accession countries in legal transformation. The unwillingness to impose competition in some important sectors in Russia and Ukraine were the main reasons that both countries have not entered the WTO. The lobby in the Russian automotive industry even launched a very successful anti-WTO campaign, entailing a preservation of protection against imports. In contrast, all EU accession countries entered the WTO, with their competition policy supervised by the WTO and the European Union.

Against this background, we can provide an overview of the current state of competition policy in accession and candidate countries. We proceed on two levels, one being the bird's-eye perspective on legal provisions for competition policy, the other the worm's perspective looking at cases of merger control, agreements, and abuses of dominant power that happened in the transition economies. For the former, we look at the EBRD's discrete numerical indicators on institutional reform provisions for competition policy and, as a control variable, the share of the private sector in the countries assessed here.[3] For the latter, two comprehensive studies provide the worm's view on the actual implementation experience of competition policy in the region. Further empirical assessment and case studies were taken from *Annual Reports* of the respective national competition offices.

Legal provisions for competition policy

The first observation from the bird's eye perspective is that the rating of competition policy falls behind the assessment of legal transition in general. This must raise concerns as, from an economic point of view, competition law can be regarded as the 'constitution of the market economy'. Peculiar circumstances of transition economies such as definition of property rights might justify this gap, but a closer look at the countries in question is needed (see Table 4.2).

Table 4.2 EBRD indicators on institutional reforms and competition policy, selected transition countries, 2001–2002

	Legal transition[a]		Competition policy[b]	Private sector share per cent[c]
	Extensiveness	Effectiveness		
Czech Republic	4–	4–	3	80
Hungary	4–	4–	3	80
Poland	3+	4–	3	75
Romania	4–	4	2+	65
Slovenia	3+	4–	3–	65

Notes:
[a] Legal transition indicators pertain to company law and are for 2002.
[b] Competition policy is for 2002.
[c] Per cent total GDP in mid-2001.
Source: EBRD (2002).

The EBRD places the Czech Republic, Hungary, and (with a small gap) Romania fairly high, although it does not give them the highest indicators for overall institutional reforms and their use in the field of company law, which would have amounted to a 4 +. Poland and Slovenia show still larger gaps. Even after more than a decade of institution building through the implantation of a well-tested system – with foreign assistance – clearly observable deficiencies remain. Moreover, the extensiveness of institutional settings and reforms in the field of company law tend to achieve lower ratings than those for the effectiveness of institutions. In those countries, the legal institutions in place do not yet satisfactorily compare with the EU benchmark, yet effectiveness is higher than the state of development of the underlying institutional framework would suggest. Both observations underscore our case that the benchmark system, the basically rule-based German model, might not have been the best solution for CEECs: apparently, a slight diversion from the benchmark grants the overall system a higher effectiveness.

In terms of anti-trust measures, state aid, etc., amalgamated into one indicator for 'competition policy', the ratings of all countries assessed here are slightly lower. This, however, is mainly due to the fiscal aid schemes granted to individual companies, frequently as a result of attempts to attract FDI. Those schemes have typically been designed to end in a foreseeable time-frame.

In terms of a cross-country comparison, the Czech Republic, Hungary, and Poland achieve the highest ratings for the transition of company laws and for delineating competition policies to guarantee a 'level playing field'. This assessment compares well with the countries' high share of private added value in total GDP. In the Czech Republic, the high rating is a recent achievement: until recently, the rating was lower due to the well-known deficiency of weaker and comparatively less effective institutions. In other words, the country appears to have achieved systemic transformation by relying less (or, at least, to a lesser degree) on the implantation of the rule-based system until recently: that gap has now been closed.

Romania, conversely, achieved the highest ratings in terms of transition of company law, yet the lowest in terms of competition policy and share of the private sector. Here, it appears, that overreliance on the alien rules-based system did not produce the desired effects and the development of a national system might be better of advice. Slovenia comes close to the assessment of Romania, but here the country's state of development is the highest among the accession countries. This seems to support to our unease with respect to the EU's 'one-size-fits-all' vision of institution building in CEECs.

Poland is stuck in the middle ground, with a competitive domestic market which has emerged not so much from privatization and FDI but rather from *de novo* establishing firms.

Experiences in implementing competition policy

For the worm's perspective, two related studies are used and supplemented by use of information provided by Annual Reports of country national competition offices. The first study is by Mavroidis and Neven (2000), which looks at the sheer number of cases of *merger control*, agreements, and abuses of dominant power in the region. The second is by Dutz and Vagliasindi (1999), which provides a more precise evaluation of the effectiveness of implementation in each accession candidate. This is evaluated in nine dimensions grouped into three categories: law enforcement,[4] competition advocacy[5] and institutional-related activities,[6] and so departs from the traditional emphasis on the number of cases processed in each country. These criteria are independent of the size of the country and have also been chosen 'so as to be amenable to unidirectional rating over time, to exclude the possibility that countries at one level of development where a particular criterion may be less relevant are penalized relative to countries at a different stage' (Dutz and Vagliasindi 1999, p. 4).

From the worm's perspective the picture above is confirmed for the two frontrunners in terms of competition policy, Hungary and Poland.

But a look at the details of competition policy and merger control, in particular, shows huge discrepancies (see Box 4.4).

Box 4.4   Examples of merger control

The following examples of merger control executed by National Competition Offices of Hungary and Poland in 1999 provide a more in-depth view on national practices:

In the Hungarian case, of the forty-six cases of merger control dealt with by the national competition authority, forty-four were initiated by the companies involved and the remaining two did not constitute explicit failures of notification. In four cases, the Competition Council of the Competition Office established that concentrations did not fall under the Competition Act, either because of insufficient turnover of market shares, or because the acquisitions were temporary and involved financial organizations – which do not qualify as concentrations to be notified.

Several of the forty-six cases involved international companies – the Hungarian law requires notification of mergers with foreign involvement according to the same rules as between pure national companies. Among the international cases, there were Ford with Volvo, Renault with Nissan, Volvo with Scania, BayWa with RWA, Exxon with Mobil, Höchst with Rhone–Poulenc, and Ramsart with Julius Meinl. The Ramsard–Meinl case, for example, was not blocked because their combined market share was clearly less than 10 per cent on the relevant Hungarian market (purchase as well as retail). Renault and Nissan command joint shares of 7 per cent on the market for passenger cars and slightly more than 12 per cent for trucks. In all the cases approved, the state authority stipulated that concentration 'did not create or strengthen a dominant position and did not impede the formation, development or continuation of the effective competition on the relevant market' (point 25 in the annual report of the Hungarian Competition Office). In other cases involving significantly higher joint market shares (e.g. Györi Keksz and Stollwerk), reaching up to 64 per cent in a narrowly defined product market, special biscuits for baking purposes market entry and import conditions were taken into consideration.

In the Polish case, the state authority investigated 1,079 cases of the 1,238 cases reported to it; 162 cases were related either to providing information to firms as to whether they were obliged to notify the office or to the Office returning approaches in cases with no legal obligation of notification. With no negative decisions, most positive decisions pertained to takeover or acquisition of stocks or shares (824), some involving the assumption of managerial functions in competing companies (twenty-nine), the acquisition or takeover of an organized part of the assets of another entrepreneur (seventeen), merger of banks (fourteen), traditional mergers of entrepreneurs (thirteen), acquisition of stocks or shares by financial institutions by professional dealers (eleven) and other, unspecified means of takeover of control (five). Contrary to the Hungarian case, the Office imposed 53 fines totalling PLN 4 million on firms for failing to notify an intention of merger on time.

First of all, Poland dealt with a far higher number of cases, in both merger control and dominance. The size of the Polish economy in comparison with the Hungarian economy will have contributed to this asymmetry, but it seems to underpin the gap in effectiveness already indicated from the bird's eye perspective. More interesting in the light of the two foregoing sections is that almost no merger was prohibited in either of these countries. The naïve observer might jump to the quick conclusion that merger control in these countries was certainly too lax. But this must be weighed against the background of the definition of the *relevant market*, and can be assessed more carefully in the Dutz–Vagliasindi study.

The same confirmation of theoretical results by empirical observations applies to the second category, namely the agreements and abuses of market dominance. Most of the cases dealt with have been agreed upon, but there remains a significant number of violations. Due to the definition of the relevant market we predict that there might be cases in which a market domination position of one or more enterprises might be justified. This explains the high number of agreements in Table 4.3. Nevertheless

Table 4.3 Anti-trust measures, selected transition countries, 1996–1999

		1996	1997	1998	1999
Merger control:					
Czech Republic	Number of cases	74	58	57	51
Hungary[a]	Number of cases	30	25	49	46
	Prohibitions	0	0	1	0
Poland	Number of cases	n.a.	1,387	1,872	1,238
	Prohibitions	1	2	1	0
Romania	Number of cases	–	13	50	173
	Prohibitions	–	n.a.	n.a.	n.a.
Slovenia	Number of cases	3	1	11	17
	Prohibitions	0	0	2	0
Agreements and abuses of dominance:					
Czech Republic	Number of cases[b]	30 + 24	27 + 5	67 + 4	54 + 13
Hungary[a]	Number of cases[b]	10 + 69	5 + 28	15 + 44	15 + 35
	Violations[b]	7 + 12	– + 4	1 + 56	6 + 7
Poland	Number of cases[c]	27 + 164	45 + 165	38 + 268	43 + 312
	Violations	79	73	124	124
Slovenia	Number of cases[d]	17 + 13 + 15	19 + 6 + 13	14 + 8 + 8	11 + 2 + 0

Notes:
[a] First column 1996–June 1997, second column June 1997–December 1997, third column 1998.
[b] The first numbers precedes are agreements, the second are proceedings abuse of dominance.
[c] The first numbers are proceedings instituted *ex officio*, the second proceedings initiated on request.
[d] The first numbers are abuse of dominant position, the second are cartel agreements and the third are vertical and horizontal agreements.

there remains a relatively high number of abuses, which indicates the effectiveness of competition policy in this field.

The Dutz–Vagliasindi study (see Table 4.4) supports the assessment that the low number of mergers prohibited in Poland and Hungary does not necessarily indicate lax merger control. On the contrary, both countries exhibit high values in all three categories: two marks out of three have been allocated to both countries in terms of their effectiveness in enforcement of regulatory activities against enterprises and state executive bodies as well as in the levying of fines, even if in only a negligible number of cases. Poland managed a 2 + for the more tentative assessment of competition advocacy while reaching only a 2 – in political independence, transparency, and the effectiveness of appeals. Nevertheless, Poland receives a slightly higher rating relative to Hungary and also the highest amongst all eighteen transition economies assessed in the study. The Czech Republic is evaluated significantly less favourably, with an overall rating of a mere 4.3 which, however, is not the lowest ranking in our sample.

The Dutz–Vagliasindi study assesses Romania more favourably with a sum of ratings of 5 – i.e. close to Hungary and Poland – in comparison to Slovenia with an overall rating of only 3.5. Considering the ratings of the EBRD, Romania appears to be more able in terms of implementation and policy effectiveness than the actual institutional framework would suggest. This is in contrast to mainly Slovenia, but also Hungary and to some degree Poland, where the institutional set-up was evaluated more preferably than implementation effectiveness.

Overall, we see a mixed picture, which is no surprise given the various start positions and different privatization policies pursued. We shall revisit this issue again in Chapter 8 when we look at competition policy from the EU membership point of view, as this perspective requires a 'one-size-for-all' policy on the EU playing field.

Table 4.4 Effectiveness of implementation of competition policy

	Law enforcement	Competition advocacy	Institutional-related activities	Sum
Czech Republic	2–	2–	1+	4.3
Hungary	2	2	2	6
Poland	2	2+	2–	6.3
Romania	2	2–	2–	5
Slovenia	1+	1–	1	3.5

Note: The numerical values have been estimated from Chart 1 in Dutz and Vagliasindi (1999). Each category reflects an assessment on a 0 (min.) to 3 (max.) scale (so that the maximum rating in the Sum column would amount to 9).

Source: Dutz and Vagliasindi (1999).

Notes

1. See Singh (2003) for a more in-depth discussion of the wider issue.
2. For this section see Hölscher and Stephan (2004).
3. It has to be noted that the EBRD's transition indicators are formed from multiple criteria assessments. They represent averages over several criteria and so hide some of the more precise facts. For our objective of a bird's-eye perspective, however, those indicators are the most reliable source of comparative information.
4. This criterion pertains to the effectiveness of enforcement activities against enterprises and state executive bodies. The third dimension assesses whether fines were actually levied in cartel cases.
5. This is measured by the effectiveness of written comments and objections concerning competition policies and related measured with a bearing on competition (infrastructure sectors and privatization policies). The third reflects education and constituency building efforts aimed at consumers and small businesses.
6. Institutional-related activities are determined by the degree of political independence of authorities, their transparency, and the effectiveness of the appeals process based on the level of adjudication.

References and further reading

Aghion, P. and W. Carlin (1997) 'Restructuring outcomes and the evolution of ownership patterns in Central and Eastern Europe', in S. Zecchini (ed.), *Lessons from the Economic Transition: Central and Eastern Europe in the 1990s* (London: Kluwer Academic Publishers), 241–63.

Bennet, J., S. Estrin, J. Maw and G. Urga (2003) 'Does the method of privatisation matter: the case of transition economies', Centre for New and Emerging Markets, Discussion Paper Series 31.

Carlin, W. and M. Landesmann, 'From theory into practice? Corporate restructuring and economic dynamisms in transition economies', *WIIW Research Reports* 240.

Dutz, M. A., Vagliasindi (1999) Competition policy implementation in transition economies: an empirical assessment, EBRD Working Paper No. 47, London.

European Bank for Reconstruction and Development (EBRD) (1997) *Transition Report 1997* (London: EBRD).

European Bank for Reconstruction and Development (EBRD) (1999) *Transition Report 1999* (London: EBRD).

European Bank for Reconstruction and Development (EBRD) (2002) *Transition Report 2002* (London: EBRD).

Estrin, S. and M. Angelucci (2003) 'Ownership, competition and enterprise performance', Centre for New and Emerging Markets, Discussion Paper Series 30.

Gomulka, S. (1985) 'Kornai's soft budget constraint and the shortage phenomenon: a criticism and restatement', *Economics of Planning* 19 (1), 1–15.

Guriev, S. and A. Rachinsky (2005) 'The role of oligarchs in Russian capitalism', *Journal of Economic Perspectives* 19(1), 131–51.

Hölscher, J. and J. Stephan. (2004) 'Competition policy in Central East Europe in the light of EU accession', *Journal of Common Market Studies*, (2), 321–45.

Hungarian Competition Office (2000).

Jurajda S. and K. Terell (2000) 'Optimal speed of transition: microevidence from the Czech Republic', Working Paper 355, University of Michigan Business School, William Davidson Institute.

Konings, J. and H. Vandenbussche (2004) 'The adjustment of financial ratios in the presence of soft budget constraints: evidence from Bulgaria', *European Accounting Review* 13(1), 131–59.

Kornai, J. (1985) 'Gomulka on the soft budget constraint: A Reply', *Economics of Planning* 19(2) 49–56.

Kornai, J., E. Maskin and G. Roland (2003) 'Understanding the soft budget constraint', *Journal of Economic Literature* 41(4), 1095–136.

Marroidis, and Neren (2000) *The International Dimension of the Antitrust Practice in Poland, Hungary and the Czech Republic*, Université de Lausanne, Ecole des HEC, Cahiers de Recherches Economiques du Départment d'Economie politique, Lausanne.

Phelps, E. S., R. Frydman, A. Rapaczynski and A. Shleifer (1993) 'Needed mechanisms of corporate governance and finance in eastern Europe', *Economics of Transition* 1, 171–207.

Schaffer, M. E. (1998) 'Do firms in transition economies have soft budget constraints? A reconsideration of concepts and evidence', *Journal of Comparative Economics* 26, 80–103.

Singh, A. (2003) 'Competition, corporate governance and selection in emerging markets', *Economic Journal* 113, 443–64.

Stiglitz, J. E. (2000) 'Whither reform? Ten years of transition', in B. Pleskovic and J. E. Stiglitz (eds), *Annual World Bank Conference on Economic Development* (Washington, DC: World Bank), 27–56.

5
Emerging Labour Markets

Chapter 5 provides an overview on the impact of transition on labour markets. It starts with some indicators describing the liberalization of labour relations. It then directs the focus on to the unemployment problem during and, possibly after, transition. The chapter introduces a model that describes the conditions for an initial rise and later fall of unemployment due to an optimal speed of restructuring the state-owned sector: the model of the optimal speed of transition (OST). Two macroeconomic concepts are used to indirectly assess the relation between market rigidities and unemployment – the Beveridge curve and Okun's law. Both concepts suggest that the present high unemployment in countries should no longer be understood as a transitional problem or a problem of too rigid markets. It is rather a matter of too little economic growth.

Supply- and demand-side liberalization

There is no official labour market in a CPE, for the government guarantees a job to everybody. In order to do that, the central planning authority defines the demand for specific jobs according to the production plan and directs people to SOEs and other organizations. Obviously, this means that not everybody can obtain the job he or she dreamed of or was qualified for. Wages were also set more or less centrally. Membership in trade unions was obligatory; union density was high, but unions had only a minor influence on income policy. The elimination of an official labour market should have ensured the non-existence of unemployment, the downside of the capitalist system, but there was an unofficial labour market, and there was hidden unemployment. Many people worked in the 'shadow economy' to earn an income higher than the official wage. SOEs hoarded labour with the intention to gain some independence from the rigid central authority. Consequently, there was a significant mismatch between qualifications of people and job occupation, contributing to inefficiency on the micro scale and imbalances on the macro scale – a constitutional defect that could be solved only by a true labour market, to be obtained by deregulation of the demand for, and supply of, labour.

But how far should deregulation go? Labour markets are subject to some regulation in all market economies, aimed at the social protection of workers, and including the application of International Labour Organization (ILO) conventions. Collective bargaining, minimum wages, etc., restrict the free labour market in most market economies. On the one side, regulation might help to ensure that wages would not fall below productivity. On the other, overregulation might increase direct and indirect labour costs and become an obstacle to full employment. Companies prefer to invest into higher productivity instead of higher employment. The European Commission, for example, had identified too much regulation on EU labour markets as the main cause for low job creation, and recommends all member countries to show more flexibility on their labour markets and restructure their social safety systems in order to lower wage costs and to increase the employment intensity of growth.

Labour market rigidity is a concept that describes the extent of regulation in market economies. One can find indicators for measuring the Employment Protection Law (EPL) and measuring the extent of active labour market policies (ALMP), and indicators describing how wage formation is organized. ELP indicators include among others the number of ILO conventions ratified by the country, the ratio of minimum wages to average labour costs in large manufacturing firms, the percentage of salaries that employers and employees have to contribute to the social security administration, or the legal number of days of maternity leave with full pay for a first-born child. ALMP indicators describe the extent of state assistance to firms for employing the long-term unemployed, or expenditures for training, etc. Indicators such as the membership of the labour movement measured as a percentage of the labour force, the ratification by the country of ILO conventions on the right to bargain collectively, describe how labour markets are organized. An indicator will fall between 1 (complete rigidity) and 0 (no rigidity). For some transition countries and 'old' EU countries Forteza and Rama (1999) found aggregate indicators values significantly higher than for industrial countries (0.39). The indicator for Germany was 0.30, and for the United Kingdom was 0.43. Among transition countries, the lowest values were found for Poland (0.45) and Russia (0.43), and the highest values for Belarus (0.64). Hungary (0.57) and Bulgaria (0.51) were in between. Another study (Cazes 2002) found that the various indicators describing the rigidities on the labour market were at a lower level than in OECD countries.

Particular strong deviations of transition countries from the industrial countries' standard appeared in the number of ILO conventions ratified and in the share of union members in the labour force (= the trade union density index) and in some protection rules. Trade union density is still higher than in the new EU member countries than in OECD countries, although trade union membership dropped significantly after transition started. Trade union density was about 49 per cent in CEE countries, but only 40 per cent in the OECD on average. Social security contributions of firms are higher than in industrial countries, and the number of days of maternity leave with full pay were seventy-five days longer on average. Minimum wages are paid in all countries, however, only in the new EU member countries are they high enough to protect against poverty (with between 20 and 50 per cent of the average monthly wage rate). Minimum wages are far below these levels in Russia and the Central Asian transition countries. All in all, labour market rigidity indicators in new EU member countries do not substantially deviate from the EU average in 2004.

The unemployment problem

After almost complete job security in the socialist area, unemployment (see Box 5.1) became a painful challenge to politicians when a deregulated labour market emerged for definitions. In 2003, the average unemployment

---

Box 5.1   EU definitions of labour market aggregates

Working age population (W): In standardized statistics the part of the population between 14 and 65 years.

Labour force (L): The number of employed and unemployed persons.

Unemployment (U): The number of job-seeking persons, registered or unregistered, in the latter case including also people below or above working age.

Unemployment rate (u): The share of unemployed in the labour force: $u = U/L$.

Employment rate (e): The share of employed in the working-age population: $e = E/W$.

Participation rate (p): The share of the labour force in the working-age population: $p = L/W = e/(1-u)$.

Public employment offices in many OECD countries also count the unfilled vacant jobs. The vacancy rate is the share of registered vacant jobs in the labour force.

rate of the new EU member countries was about 14 per cent, with Poland about 19 per cent and Hungary 6 per cent. Unemployment rates were low in China, some Central Asian successor states of the Soviet Union, and in Belarus. In China, exceptionally high output growth secured job opportunities in the private and quasi-private sector outside agriculture[1] when agricultural reforms set many people free. In Central Asia and in Belarus, state subsidies and weak transition advances contributed to low unemployment rates.

Unemployment rates in the European transition countries, in particular in the new EU member states, are even higher than in the EU-15 (Table 5.1). They are a matter of concern for EU-15 politicians, for they fear an excessive pressure on emigration from these countries. High unemployment rates also partly mirror low employment rates. The average employment rate fell from 68 per cent in 1990 to 56 per cent in new member countries in 2003, while it was about 61 per cent in the EU-15. The ambitious objective of the EU's *Lisbon strategy* was to become the most dynamic growth region of world economy by 2010, among other things achieving an employment rate of 70 per cent on average. Low employment in new member countries makes this aim an unrealistic dream.

Table 5.1 Employment and unemployment rates[a] 2003 (in per cent)

	Employment rate[b]	Unemployment rate[c]
EU-15 average	61.2	8.7
New member countries Average	56.2	14.4
Czech Republic	68.0	7.5
Estonia	65.1	10.1
Hungary	56.4	5.7
Latvia	63.1	10.5
Lithuania	62.0	12.9
Poland	51.1	19.3
Slovak Republic	57.4	17.4
Slovenia	63.5	6.6
Bulgaria	52.5	13.6
Romania	57.6	6.6
Russia	Not available	2.3[d]

Notes:
[a] Labour Force Survey data.
[b] in per cent of population aged 15–64.
[c] in per cent of the labour force (age 15+).
[d] Registered.

Sources: EU (2004); UN–ECE (2005).

Increasing unemployment rates do not fully illustrate the job destruction during transition. Governments attempted to mitigate the impact of transition on the labour market, for they feared social unrest and the disreputation of transition. Some governments imposed schemes for early retirement, the Polish government sent almost 1 million people into early retirement in the early 1990s. About 1 million of the labour force disappeared in Hungary from the statistics, consisting mainly of old age pensioners who had been formerly employed. Nor do falling employment rates give a complete picture of job destruction. In some countries, cuts in unemployment benefits reduced the incentive for the unemployed to register. Unemployed joined the *hidden reserve* (= people who would like to work but saw no opportunity and, therefore, did not register) or people who took a job in the shadow economy. In some countries (such as the Czech Republic), the government softened the budget constraints on SOEs – a policy prevalent in Russia from the very beginning of transition.

Emigration contributed to lowered unemployment, above all in the Baltic states. Estonia lost 14 per cent of its population between 1990 and 2004. More than half of this loss can be attributed to emigration, above all the withdrawal of the Russian military and discrimination of against the remaining Russian population. Emigration reduces the labour force and the working-age population by the same number of people; however, since the former is smaller than the latter, the participation rate will also shrink. What happened in the Baltic States was that employed persons emigrated, and the employment rate fell, but the unemployment rate increased (this can be seen by using the definitions in Box 5.1). The participation rate increased in the old EU between 1992 and 2003, while it fell in new member countries between (Figure 5.1).

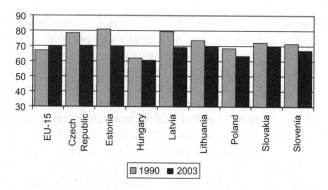

Figure 5.1 Participation rates in the labour force: per cent of working age population (15–64), 1990 and 2003

Sources: EU Commission (2004); own calculations.

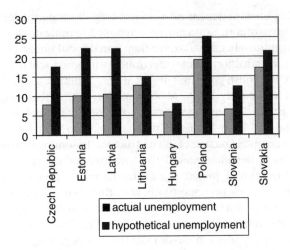

Figure 5.2   Employment rates, in per cent, at 1990 and 2003 participation rates

Figure 5.2 clearly illustrates the drama in transition countries. Assuming a participation rate of 1990 – that is, without early retirement schemes, registration rigidities, and emigration – unemployment rates would have turned out to be far higher than were actually reported. Poland, for example, would had reported an unemployment rate of 25 per cent instead of 19 per cent in 2003. Estonia would have shown an unemployment rate of more than 20 per cent without emigration instead of 10 per cent!

The optimal speed of transition

Full employment in market economies means, by common agreement, an unemployment rate between 3 per cent and 5 per cent of the labour force. One can imagine that unemployment needs to be higher in transition countries than in mature market economies, for the private sector would not make progress without leavers in the state-owned sector. But do we know anything about the 'optimal' rate of unemployment during transition due to purely institutional determinants, and assuming no major mistakes in stabilization policy? The most influential theory linking unemployment dynamics to institutional changes is the *Optimal Speed of Transition (OST)* theory. This theory explains that unemployment, along with restructuring/privatization of SOEs, is an important prerequisite for job creation in the emerging private sector. Unemployment will depress the wage rate below the private sector's marginal productivity and improve private profit expectations. This is crucial for the rise of the private sector in the absence of an efficient financial sector providing capital and credit. However, there is a threshold of unemployment, any restructuring policy should be careful not to pass it. Otherwise, the private sector's ability to create new jobs would weaken, and job destruction might even emerge in the private sector. The unemployment rate would tend to increase instead of decline by the completion of transition. Where the threshold is depends on the determinants of the speed of restructuring.

In their seminal work on the optimal speed of transition Phillippe Aghion and Oliver Blanchard (1994) provide the model (see Appendix 1 p. 90) for a formal presentation of the basic idea). The model explains that the private sector is able to create new jobs when an initial increase of unemployment lowers the wage rate and increases the sector's profitability, all other determinants (for example, aggregate demand) given. However, when unemployment becomes too high, higher social taxes financing the unemployed might compensate for the profitability gain. Unemployment might become even so high that job destruction was not restricted to the state-owned and privatised sector, but spread also to the private sector. The rate of unemployment jeopardizing the private sector's job creation depends on the speed of restructuring in the state-owned and privatised sector. This speed can be under the government's control, but it may also depend on the *method of privatization*, offering many possibilities to the workers to influence it.

Empirical research on models on (un)employment suffers from weak data availability and has often remained primarily a theoretical exercise (Haltiwanger, Lehmann and Terell 2003). Although some author have tried to rely on empirical evidence, their work has not been able to apply the usual formal tests. A basic problem here is the *singularity of transition*, which restricts the number of observations. Therefore, economists have not found clear answer as to whether unemployment rates in transition countries reflect failures in the transition concept, or a too high a speed of transition and may be expected to decline over time when transition finally comes to an end.

However, there is one piece of evidence that is at least mildly persuasive. Figure 5.3 depicts the example of Poland. Total employment fell by 2.7 million between 1989 and 2002, of which two-third were released from industry, although private firms created 1 million jobs. The unemployment rate was about 20 per cent in 2003. The X-axis marks the unemployment rate in per cent of the labour force, the Y-axis private job creation in per cent of private jobs in industry and job destruction in the

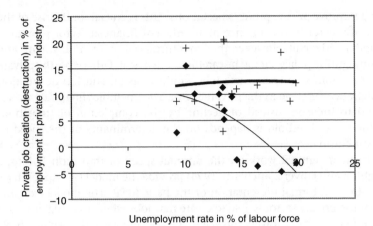

Figure 5.3 Job destruction and job creation, Poland, 1990–2002

Sources: Eurostat (Ameco database); Central Statistical Office of Poland, Rocznik Statistyczny, various years; own calculations.

state industry in per cent of state jobs. The points report all the annual matches between the unemployment rate and *private job creation* in the thirteen years of transition. The lower curve is the trend line, which links all these matches. The crosses report all matches between job *destruction in state industry* and the unemployment rate, and thus the inflow into unemployment from the state sector. The upper line stems from these matches, and approximates the speed of transition; it is the trend of job destruction in state industry. The picture shows an increasing gap between the speed of inflow from state industry into unemployment and the speed of outflow to private industry from unemployment with increasing unemployment rates. The speed of state sector reconstruction seems to have been too fast for private job creation.

Of course, one should not be too eager to interpret this pattern as evidence for the OST model. There may be alternative explanations for high unemployment – for example, the strong losses in aggregate demand at the beginning of transition. The emergence of international financial crises in the second half of the 1990s and the response of the Polish government and monetary authorities in damping down domestic aggregate demand to mitigate such crisis are also relevant. Furthermore, there is the issue of *labour market rigidity*. Too much regulation might be a severe obstacle to the private sector to engage workers released from the state-owned sector.

The Beveridge curve

A macroeconomic summary indicator of many kinds of labour market rigidity is the location and movement of the so-called *Beveridge curve*, named after the wartime report of Sir William Beveridge (1879–1963) of 1944. The curve is a downward-sloping relation between the vacancy rate and the unemployment rate (Figure 5.4).

The dashed curves in Figure 5.4 have a negative slope because vacant jobs are easier to fill, the more unemployed workers there are for employers to choose among. In a perfectly flexible labour market, where wages adjusted so that every part of the labour market had adequate employment opportunities, vacant jobs, and unemployed workers could not coexist. In this case, the curve would be a line coinciding with the axes of the diagram. However, since there are rigidities in the labour

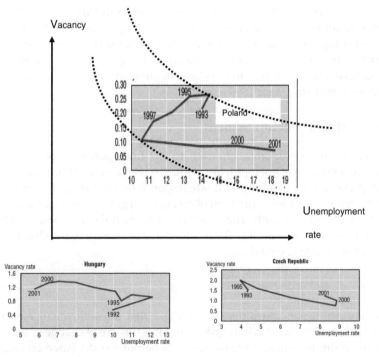

Figure 5.4 The Beveridge curve: Poland, 1993–2001
Source: OECD (2003).

market, the curve has the form presented in the *U–V* space in Figure 5.4. *Employment protection legislation*, which consists of the regulations determining the level of employment security as mentioned earlier can affect matching efficiency. The *benefit system* directly affects the readiness of the unemployed to fill vacancies. *Active labour market polices* may facilitate the matching between unemployed and vacancies. Finally, *limited geographical mobility* constitutes another barrier to matching job seekers with available jobs. A curve that lies far to the left (i.e. close to the vacancy axis) indicates that unemployed workers are easily matched to vacant jobs, while a curve far to the right indicates severe mismatch and high equilibrium unemployment. A rightward shift of the curve means more labour market rigidity responsible for higher unemployment. However, limitations in the availability and quality of data on vacancies present considerable difficulties for conducting an empirical analysis of these patterns. Figure 5.4 also presents the shifts of the Beveridge curve that the OECD (2003) estimated for Poland, the Czech Republic, and Hungary. It suggests fewer market rigidities between 1993 and 1998 for Poland. Between 1998 and 2001, Poland's labour market seems to have moved on the same Beveridge curve, indicating a negligible impact of market rigidity on unemployment. The curves for the Czech Republic and Hungary present different pictures. Hungary's curve shows an impressive leftward shift; in the Czech Republic the curve seems to have moved rightward since 1999.

Growth and unemployment

Another macroeconomic approach to the unemployment problem is the analysis of the unemployment–growth relationship. If this relationship exists, the unemployment rate responds to a change in the growth rate of output, either in the form of cyclical changes or simply in the form of a higher growth path. The legacy of high unemployment rates might then be overcome by less fiscal and monetary restrictions. One may estimate a simple equation:

$$\Delta U_t = \alpha_0 - \alpha_1 y_t + \mu \qquad (5.1)$$

where ΔU_t is the first difference of the actual unemployment rate in period t against the previous period, and y_t is the rate of change of actual GDP in this period. α_0 is the trend rate of output growth, based on long-run productivity and technology trends, and contributes to an increase in unemployment. α_1 is the unemployment elasticity of output variations.

The expected sign is negative, for output growth should reduce unemployment. μ is the disturbance term. A test for (5.1) reveals first and above all whether this relationship exists in transition countries. If so, the coefficients allow us to estimate the necessary growth rates: The relation $1/\alpha_1$ says how much growth above trend growth is necessary to reduce the unemployment rate by 1 percentage point. The coefficient can serve as an indirect measure for the institutional ability of an economy to transform growth into employment. The higher the coefficient, the fewer the institutional obstacles, including market rigidities. The relation α_0/α_1 illustrates the *unemployment threshold* of growth – that is, how much additional growth is necessary to avoid a further increase of the unemployment rate due to long-run productivity progress (Figure 5.5).

Equation (5.1) is one of the forms of test for Okun's law (Box 5.2). The law is the empirically robust relationship between changes in output and employment in market economies. The empirical confirmation of the law simply says that (un)employment responds to GDP changes, which is typical for market economies but not for socialist planned economies. This response is also not expected during early transition, when unemployment is the result of institutional/political changes and macroeconomic shocks. If equation (5.1) holds we may assume that transition is no longer playing a role in current changes in the unemployment rate, and that high unemployment is a legacy of former transition shocks.

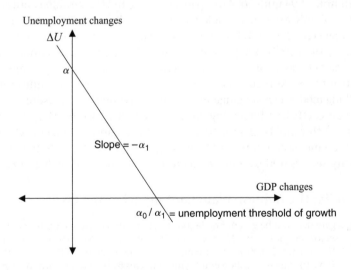

Figure 5.5 The relationship between unemployment and GDP changes

---

Box 5.2   Okun's law

The American economist Arthur M. Okun (1928–1980) found a stable relationship between the output gap and the deviation of the unemployment rate from its equilibrium value for the US economy in 1962:

$$Y_{gap} = -\theta U_{dev} \tag{5.2}$$

where the output gap is measured as the cyclical deviation of actual from potential output. θ is the so-called Okun coefficient (Okun 1962). Compared with the empirical form in Figure 5.5, the curve runs through the origin. In Okun's research, the coefficient took a value of about 0.3 for the United States. Hence, a 3 per cent deviation of actual output from potential output was related to a decline in the unemployment rate of about 1 per cent. Later empirical research used the inverse relationship and tested changes in the actual unemployment and growth rates, when potential output and equilibrium unemployment cannot be calculated. Empirical research uses sometimes the Non-Accelerating Inflation Rate of Unemployment (NAIRU) as the equilibrium unemployment rate. Other research tries to estimate potential output by taking the trend of actual output. Okun himself used a weaker form of this law, which relates changes in the actual unemployment rate to changes in actual output. This approach tests for the simple responsiveness of unemployment to output changes. In most market economies, the Okun coefficient turned out to be between 1 and 0.1.

Indeed, using annualized data on registered unemployment and GDP growth from 1994 until 2004 in a panel of the eight EU accession countries of 2004. Okun's law seems to hold (Gabrisch and Buscher, 2005). Izyumov and Vahaly (2002) found similar results for advanced transition countries. However, the link is not present in the early stages of transition, and other models such as OST seem better to explain unemployment. Results for the Okun coefficient seem also to be conform to indicators describing moderate market rigidity in transition countries. The estimations found an coefficient increasing with progress in transition. The unemployment thresholds of growth were rising in most countries, which reflects an increasing impact of technology progress in hitherto low-productivity sectors (for example, agriculture in Poland), partly due to FDI.

Appendix: the Aghion–Blanchard model of the OST

Let aggregate demand be given. The labour force consists of state employment E, private sector employment N, and unemployment U. Normalized to one, $E + N + U = 1$ with U being the unemployment rate. In the CPE, $E = 1$ and $N = U = 0$. With transition, state employment begins to shrink. The driving force is the imposition of 'hard' budget constraints by fiscal and/or monetary restriction. Privatized firms are forced to restructure and to reduce their staff in order to achieve profitability comparable to that of the private sector. Let the speed of restructuring in the former state firms s be a variable under the control of the government, so that

$$dE/dt = -s \tag{5A1.1}$$

This is the basic version of the model, which disregards the impact of workers in state or privatized enterprises on the restructuring process, an impact which depends on the privatization method.

The reduction of E flows into unemployment. The size of this reduction depends, with given s, from the remaining stock of workers in state-owned firms $0 \leq \lambda \leq 1$. Hence, $(1-\lambda)$ is the proportion of state workers who lose their job during the process of restructuring.

The private sector hires new workers from unemployment. With increasing unemployment from the state sector, and with job creation H in the private sector, the unemployment rate develops according to

$$dU/dt = s(1 - \lambda) - H \tag{5A1.2}$$

Private job creation is given by

$$H = a(y - z - w) \tag{5A1.3}$$

where a is a parameter, y is the constant average product of labour in the private sector, w is the wage in the private sector, and z are taxes per worker (= indirect wage costs). Equation (5A1.3) demonstrates that job creation depends on profit per worker. Private sector wages depend on labour market conditions:

$$w = b + c\ (r + H/U) \tag{5A1.4}$$

where b is the unemployment benefit, r is the interest rate, and H/U is the ratio of hires to unemployment. The higher unemployment is, the lower is the private sector wage. This equation is derived from efficiency wage considerations, where firms pay wages to ensure that the rate of being employed exceeds the value of being unemployed; therefore, $c \geq 0$.

Taxes per worker are collected to ensure benefits for the unemployed. With a balanced budget, the fiscal expenditure for unemployment (Ub) equals the fiscal revenues from state and private workers $(E+N)z$, or

$$Ub = (1 - U)z \tag{5A1.5}$$

illustrating that higher unemployment leads to higher taxes. Private job creation depends on unemployment through two channels, wages and taxes, as in (5A1.3). First, unemployment depresses wages according to (5A1.4) and increases job creation. Second, unemployment increases taxes per worker through (5A1.5) and decreases job creation. From (5A1.2), (5A1.3), and (5A1.4) one receives by solving for H:

$$H = a\left[\frac{U}{U + ca}\right]\left[y - rc - \frac{1}{1-U}b\right] \equiv f(U) \tag{5A1.6}$$

This equation puts together both effects. The first term in brackets is the positive effect on job creation by lower wages, and the second term in brackets is the negative effect by higher taxes.

Figure 5A1.1 plots $H = f(U)$ as a function of U. With zero unemployment, the wage rate is equal to the average product y in the private sector; no incentive for job creation exists. Remember that we assume a given aggregate demand and the absence of lending activities of the financial sector. When unemployment increases in the first stage of transition, the effect that dominates initially is the direct effect on wages ($w < y$), so that private job creation increases. When unemployment becomes sufficiently large, the effect on taxes exceeds the effect on wages, and private job creation declines. As unemployment gets large enough, wages and contributions exceed the average product of labour, leading to the disappearance of the private sector. Thus, at low unemployment, an increase in unemployment leads to more job creation; at high unemployment, higher unemployment leads to less job creation. The fiscal burden might even become so large that both the new and the privatized sectors become unprofitable and close down.

If we draw the flow from restructuring into unemployment as a horizontal line at $s(1-\lambda)$ there appear two equilibriums. If the speed of labour-shedding in the restructuring sector is less than private job creation, A becomes a stable equilibrium. In U_A the inflow into unemployment from the state sector will be

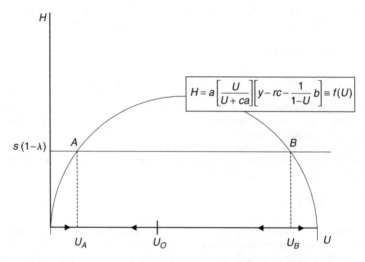

Figure 5A1.1   The dynamics of state job reduction and private job creation

completely absorbed by the private sector. So far, the initial unemployment rate U_0 is below U_B, unemployment tends to return to the stable equilibrium, and U_A. If initial unemployment U_0 is at the right of U_B, then private job creation will be insufficient to avoid a further increase in unemployment, and the private sector may probably collapse.

Note

1. This sector includes SMEs and excludes collective firms run by private persons, foreign-invested companies, small unincorporated businesses, individually invested corporatized enterprises, and partnerships. There has actually been no privatization of state-owned firms until now.

References and further reading

Aghion, P. and O. J. Blanchard (1994). 'On the speed of transition in Central Europe', in Stanley Fischer and Julio Rotemberg, (eds), *NBER Macroeconomics Annual 1994*, 283–320.

Castanheira, M. and G. Roland (2000) 'The optimal speed of transition: a general equilibrium analysis', *International Economic Review* 41 (1), 219–39.

Cazes, S. (2002). 'Do labour market institutions matter in transition economies: an analysis of labour market flexibility in the late nineties', International Institute for Labour Studies, *Discussion Paper* 140.

Döpke, J. (2001) 'The "employment intensity" of growth in Europe', *Kiel Working Paper* 1021, Kiel Institute of World Economics.

European Bank for Reconstruction and Development (EBRD) (2000) *Transition Report 2000* (London: EBRD).

European Bank for Reconstruction and Development (EBRD) (2004) *Transition Report 2004* (London: EBRD).

EU Commission (2004) *Employment in Europe 2004. Recent Trends and Prospects*, manuscript (August 2004), Brussels, available at http://europa.eu.int/comm/employment_social/employment_analysis/eie/eie2004_forew_toc_sum_en.pdf.

Forteza, A. and M. Rama (1999) 'Labor market "rigidity" and the success of economic reforms across more than hundred countries', World *Bank Policy Research Working Paper* 2521.

Gabrisch. and H. Buscher (2005) 'Unemployment dynamics in new EU member countries: a test for Okun's law', *IWH-Discussion Papers* 5.

Garibaldi, P. and Z. Brixiova (1997) 'Labor market institutions and unemployment dynamics in transition economies', IMF *Working Paper* 97/137 (Washington, DC: IMF).

Haltiwanger, J., H. Lehmann and K. Terrell (2003), 'Job creation and job destruction in transition countries', *Economics of Transition* 11(2), 205–219.

Izyumov, A. and J. Vahaly (2002) 'The unemployment–output tradeoff in transition economies: does Okun's law apply?', *Economics of Planning* 35 (4), 317–31.

Landesmann, M., H. Vidovic and T. Ward (2005) 'Economic restructuring and labour market developments in the new EU member states', WIIW-*Research Reports*, No 312 (Vienna: Institute for Comparative Economic Studies).

Nesporova, A. (2002) 'Why unemployment remains so high in Central and Eastern Europe', Employment Paper 2002/43 (Geneva: ILO).

OECD (2003) *OECD Employment Outlook: 2003. Towards More and Better Jobs, Chapter 1* (Paris: OECD).

Okun, A. M. (1962) 'Potential GDP: its measurement and significance', *Proceedings of the Business and Economics Statistics Section*, American Statistical Association, 98–103.

Prachowny, M. F. J. (1993) 'Okun's law: theoretical foundations and revised estimates', *The Review of Economics and Statistics* 75, 331–36.

UN–ECE (2005) *Economic Survey of Europe* 1 (Geneva: United Nations Economic Commission for Europe).

WIIW (Wiener Institut für Internationale Wirtschaffs Vergleiche) (various dates) *Monthly Data Bank* (The Vienna Institute for Comparative Economic Studies) Vienna.

6
Opening towards the World

Chapter 6 distinguishes between the benefits of an open economy and the specific risks of opening the economy. A first challenge to transition policy is how to mitigate the shocks on production stemming from getting distorted price relations right after the removal of trade controls and selective protection. The chapter explains why, and how, output declines when opening leads to a massive adjustment of price relations via a higher price level as well as via changing the positive into the negative value added of industries. The chapter further discusses whether, and how, to use the exchange rate of the currency as a non-selective tool for protecting the economy. The chapter also illustrates that the exchange rate tool becomes more or less ineffective when the government lifts capital controls. The exchange rate depends on free capital flows, and undesired capital movements have their own impact on output via the exchange rate and the financial system.

The open and the opening economy

Basically, the socialist CPE was a *closed economy*, although each socialist country exported and imported commodities. Imports followed the planning authority's needs for certain quantities of raw material and energy, and some new technology, and exports served to earn foreign exchange income. In the ideal world of central planning, trade tends to be balanced, and temporary imbalances are covered by short-term trade credit. Prices and tariffs do not play an important role in planning, and domestic price relations tend to diverge from international relations. Because of the passive role money play in the domestic economy, the currency not convertible. There is no unique exchange rate for the currency, but administratively set industry-specific conversion rates. International capital movements have restricted to short-term credit, initially not in money but rather in kind. Reality was somewhat different from the ideal world. For countries that were not able to make use of the benefits of free international trade, relations with the world were as suboptimal as domestic production. Most socialist countries became heavily indebted in their later years, due to the fact that domestic producers were cut off from external markets and isolated from technical progress and innovation. The attempt of governments to service the foreign debt by reducing consumption and even investment contributed to the political breakdown of the socialist system.

There were some specifics factors in the external position of the countries. First, with the exception of the Soviet Union, all countries were small countries, with few mineral resources. They had to produce manufactured goods with domestic labour and capital and imported raw material and energy. If they had been open economies they would have to act as *price takers* for manufactured goods on world markets. The Soviet Union (and today Russia), on the other hand, was and is a large country with abundant resources such as like iron or energy, and had a certain influence on international prices. Both the Soviet Union and the region of smaller CEECs formed a specific group of economic cooperation, the Council of Mutual Economic Assistance (CMEA). Mutual trade was conducted according to the partly synchronized central plans of the countries. The typical feature of this kind of 'specialization' was that the Soviet Union delivered the energy needed at a price lower than world market prices, in exchange for manufactured goods.

For any economy, the basic macroeconomic link between output and the external sector can be written as:

$$Y \equiv C + I + G + (X - M) \tag{6.1}$$

where Y is output or GDP, C private consumer demand, I demand for investment goods, G public consumer demand, X export, and M import demand. $(X-M)$ is the balance of trade (BT). A trade deficit reduces aggregate output. The step from an identity to a model, which explains this link, is done by including factors which have an impact on export and import demand. In an economy open only for trade, without any capital movements, *relative prices* and the *real exchange rate* matter. The notation of 'relative prices' means the domestic price relation–that is, how expensive an input (say, energy) is in relation to another input (say, some intermediate good). But in the context of international trade, the more interesting question is how this domestic relative price deviates from the world market relative price. Obviously, the *level of protection* plays an important role, as well as the *similarity* and *quality* of traded goods. We write the relation between the vector of domestic and foreign prices of all goods $i = 1,..., n$ as

$$P_i^d / P_i^f$$

and the real exchange rate as E^r and get:

$$BT = X(P_i^d/P_i^f, E) - M(P_i^d/P_i^f, E) \tag{6.2}$$

Note that in the open economy, the relative domestic prices of goods tend to converge towards the relative prices of foreign goods, when they are identical and have the same quality. This is called the 'law of one price' and (see below p. 98) may include a general increase in the domestic price level under certain circumstances convergence. Obviously, the impact of 'getting prices right' on output depends on the degree of price distortions. With respect to the CMEA framework, the initial price distortions were huge. The smaller members imported cheap Soviet raw material and energy below world market prices, and the Soviet Union imported manufactured goods. The relative price for the latter, measured in material and energy inputs, was above the world market relation. This included an income gain for the smaller CMEA countries and an income transfer from the Soviet Union, which vanished after trade was liberalized. What is more, the higher prices for energy imports entailed a higher inflation rate, lower real incomes and a negative impact on aggregate demand.

The second determinant of trade and output is the *real exchange rate* of the domestic currency. A depreciation of the exchange rate has no impact on relative prices, but on output via domestic demand and external competitiveness.

The first challenge for transition countries was thus how to mitigate output losses, when almost all relative prices were distorted. The abundant theoretical and empirical literature demonstrates the welfare effects of free trade by assuming internal and external equilibrium of the economies considered, but the CPE was far from equilibrium. The move from a closed and heavily distorted to an open economy is the way to this equilibrium state, but establishment of equilibrium at one stroke is possible only at high economic cost. Foreign competition may turn out to be destructive, for domestic industries may not be able to adjust to new relative prices. The best example is East Germany. Akerlof *et al.* (1991) analysed how the sudden inclusion of a CPE in the EU Single Market contributed to the breakdown of industry. Hence, should trade be liberalized completely and at one stroke or rather step by step?

The issue becomes more complicated when trade opening is accompanied by lifting controls on international capital movements. The link between the domestic economy (output) and the external sector runs via the *balance of payments* (BOP). In such a completely open economy, the BOP identity holds:

$$BOP \equiv CA + NCF \equiv 0 \tag{6.3}$$

where CA is the balance of the current account and NCF net capital inflows. The BT is one component of the current account – the latter includes further net income flows (interest payments, profit repatriation) and transfers.[1] It is important to note that the BOP is always 0, and that a NCF induces a negative change in the current account balance, either as a higher trade deficit or as interest payments. The stock of all NCFs is the external debt of the country. In the CMEA framework, without factor mobility, the NCF as well as interest payments and other transfers were almost 0, and the BOP narrowed more or less to the BT. But in the final stage, socialist countries became heavily indebted against market economies: trade deficits were financed with long-term credit first, and then with short-term credit.

While the impact of capital flows on commodity price relations is negligible, the impact on the real exchange rate, the price level and the domestic interest rate level is crucial. With NCF the exchange rate appreciates in real terms (and in nominal terms if it is flexible). Each NCF expands the money supply and leads to higher inflation and lower interest rates, which in turn causes the trade balance to deteriorate. Hence, a second major challenge to transition economies results: on the one hand, free capital movements promise access to financing for investment. On the other hand, the exchange rate as well as the money supply is no longer under the control of the government. The crucial problem is that excessive capital movements can destabilize the economy. Capital flight might may deplete the country of necessary financial means. How to protect the economy against undesired capital movements? Should the capital account of the economy be liberalized, when the financial sector is weak and monetary policy effectiveness restricted?

How to assess the impact of those undesired capital flows on output and currency stability?

Price convergence and aggregate demand

Two studies revealed that the price level in the closed socialist economies was below their international level at the beginning of transition (Coorey, Mecagni and Offerdal 1996; Koen and De Masi 1997). The combination of price and trade liberalization had an important impact on the general price level of the transition economy, and on its output. Koen and De Masi (1997) found for transition countries that domestic prices of tradables in CEE countries converged quickly toward the higher international level after liberalization. They found a clear positive correlation between relative price variability and inflation. This applies mainly to tariffs of services and prices of food. This effect is to distinguish from the corrective inflation after price liberalization, because corrective inflation is due to a macroeconomic imbalance, while the convergence of price relations and the price level towards the level and relation in market economies finds its background in distorted price structures. This effect is to be distinguished from exchange rate specifics, for the currency in which relative prices are measured does not play a role. Price convergence emerges only when both domestic and international prices are compared in the same currency. The effect on output is straightforward: The higher the price level, the lower is the real income in the economy, for the nominal income level is given. With lower real income, aggregate demand (consumption) will decline, and actual output will follow.

Relative price shocks and value added

Transition started with a shift from quantitative import restriction to tariffs, and with a lowering of those tariffs. In the then Czechoslovakia, the average tariff level amounted to 8 per cent in 1991 and to only 3 per cent in 1993. The average tariff fell to 4 per cent in Poland 1990, and in Hungary to 7 per cent in 1991. These levels were even below the average level the European Union demanded on imports at this time. Following the quick and comprehensive liberalization of trade in fifteen small transition countries of Europe, trade balances in most of them turned into, and remained in, deficit. Figure 6.1 illustrates how

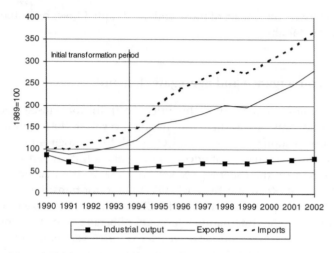

Figure 6.1 Industrial output and external trade, 1990–2002 (1989 = 100), in transition countries[a]

Note: [a] Mean value of: Albania, Bosnia & Herzegovina, Bulgaria, Croatia, Czech Republic, Estonia, Hungary, Latvia, Lithuania, Poland, Romania, Serbia & Montenegro, Slovakia, Slovenia, Macedonia.

Source: UN–ECE (2003).

the gap between import and export widened in East European transition countries between 1990 and 2002. Figure 6.1 also shows that industrial output declined by nearly 50 per cent on average.[2] In Poland and Estonia, where the move to free trade was almost complete in the first years of transition, the output decline turned out to be particularly severe. East Germany (not included in Figure 6.1), in particular, demonstrates this: industrial output was 40 per cent of the 1989 level in 1994.

Certainly, the size of output decline cannot be completely explained by short-run trade shocks or an increase in the overall price level. In some countries, civil war turbulence contributed (the successor states of FYR), or the break-up of some states (Czechoslovakia: the Czech Republic and the Slovak Republic, the Soviet Union: Baltic states) exerted a negative impact on output as well as trade. But it seems important to relate the joint output breakdown and the opening issue to the breakdown of the CMEA itself. Assume a small socialist economy, whose industry produced finished goods and used material inputs for that production imported from the Soviet Union, and only domestic labour. Assume further that imported material inputs are used domestically at domestic currency prices. Finished goods are import substitutes, they can be sold at prices higher than their foreign counterparts within the CMEA. Selling them outside the CMEA meant a lower world market price. When the Soviet Union suddenly stopped supplying cheap energy (and other raw materials) to the smaller countries in 1991–1992, the finished goods industries of the partner countries produced negative value added, for the costs of material inputs in terms of world market prices increased at an extent that consumed all the positive value added at former domestic, but distorted prices. The major distortion was in the relative price of energy against manufactured goods. Because of the inability to adjust the relative price of energy to labour in a short time after the break down of the CMEA and with the lifting of all import protection, those industries with a negative value added simply collapsed. The Appendix (p. 108) captures the main aspects in a more formalized way.

The output collapse in many industries opened the way to a more gradual move to free trade, above all in trade with the European Union (see Gácz 1994; Csaba 1996). Some countries introduced temporary taxes on imports. Those countries that started free trade negotiations with the European Union increased the average tariff in order to have something to negotiate. A milestone was the European Agreements, including the gradual introduction of a free trade area (FTA) by 2002. This agreement included an asymmetric mutual opening: the Union abandoned all quotas and tariffs, the candidate countries were to follow with some delay. Some countries even imposed new tariffs on the import of cars: Western automotive investors pressured the governments of these countries, otherwise they would refuse to invest directly.

The exchange rate as a tool for trade policy

The limits of devaluation

While tariffs offer the option for selective protection, the exchange rate is a tool for general protection of the government. The aim of using this tool is to cause the real exchange rate to devalue and to improve competitiveness for exported goods and import substitution. Assume closed capital accounts and a nominal exchange rate fixed by the government. A devaluation of the fixed peg would cause the real exchange rate to follow only when the domestic inflation rate remained lower than the rate of devaluation. This was possible, for the devaluation raised the prices of imported goods, which were only a part of goods consumed or processed in the economy. The money supply responded passively and ensured a once-and-for-all increase in the inflation rate. Thus, the exchange rate as a trade policy tool was effective only in the environment of non-liberalised capital flows. In the context of an early-stage transition economy (with capital controls) a heavy devaluation in real terms was the only option to avoid a collapse of production and increasing external debt after lifting almost all the quantitative trade barriers. The initial nominal devaluation turned out to be high in some countries (Poland, Czechoslovakia); the benchmark was the black market exchange rate.

It is important to understand that a devaluation of the exchange rate can improve the trade balance only if the price elasticity of both exports and imports is sufficiently high – that is the Marshall–Lerner condition is fulfilled, or: the sum of both elasticities needs to be larger than unity (see Box 6.1).

Box 6.1   The Marshall–Lerner condition

Assume that the nominal exchange rate E expresses the number of domestic currency units that will buy one foreign currency unit. The exchange rate represents strictly the relation of the domestic price level for tradable goods P to the world market price P^*: $P = EP^*$. Assume further that with a constant domestic price the foreign price of an export item declines with a depreciation of E, and that there is positive response of foreign demand for exports. We define the response of the export volume X to a nominal depreciation as price elasticity of exports: $\eta_x = dX/X : dE/E > 0$ that is, the export volume will increase when the nominal exchange rate depreciates. Similarly, we can write for the response of the import volume:

$$\eta_M = \frac{dM}{M} : \frac{dE}{E} < 0$$

where the demand for imported goods declines with a nominal devaluation, which leads to a higher domestic price level of the imported good. We write the BT in terms of domestic currency units as:

$$BT = PX - P^*EM, \text{ and differentiate it against a change of } E: \quad (6.4)$$

$$\frac{dB}{dE} = P\frac{dX}{dE} - P^*M - P^*\frac{E}{dE}dM. \text{ Dividing by } M \text{ yields:} \quad (6.5)$$

Continued

Box 6.1 Continued

$$\frac{\left(\frac{dBT}{dE}\right)}{M} = P\frac{dX}{dE}\frac{1}{M} - P* - P*\frac{E}{dE}\frac{dM}{M} \qquad (6.6)$$

When the right-hand first term is enlarged with X/X, and P is substituted by $P*E$, one obtains:

$$= P*\frac{E}{de}\frac{dX}{X}\frac{X}{M} - P* - P*\frac{E}{dE}\frac{dM}{M} \qquad (6.7)$$

We define $M/X = u$, divide both sides by $P*$, and insert the definitions for the price elasticity from above:

$$dBT = \eta_X\frac{1}{u} - 1 - \eta_M = \left(\eta_X\frac{1}{u}\right) - 1 - \eta_M \qquad (6.8)$$

dBT is now the change of the real trade balance in terms of import units. The BT will improve after a depreciation when the right-hand expression is larger than zero:

$$\eta_x - u(1 + \eta_M) > 0 \qquad (6.9)$$

When $M = X$, and trade is initially balanced, $u = 1$, we obtain the traditional form of the *Marshall–Lerner* condition: $|\eta_x + \eta_M| > 1$. Remember that the price elasticity of the import demand is less than 0, and the minus sign in front of the bracket in (6.9) turns into a positive. Equation (6.9) says that the sum of both export and import elasticity needs to be larger than 1 with balanced trade. If there were a initial trade deficit with $u > 1$ we obtain

$$\left|\eta_x\frac{1}{u} + \eta_M\right| > 1 \qquad (6.10)$$

What we can see here is that the higher the deficit is the more difficult the condition is fulfilled. On the other hand, from (6.7), the inflationary impact of a devaluation shrinks with a rising deficit.

Earlier empirical analysis by the IMF revealed that the Marshall–Lerner condition is usually met in the medium and long run, but not in the short period. A real depreciation causes the BT to deteriorate immediately after the devaluation. One of the reasons is that current exports and imports in terms of the new exchange rate follow contracts of earlier periods, still agreed on the basis of the old exchange rates In the medium and long run, export and import demands adjust gradually to price changes. This is called the '*J-curve*' effect of a real depreciation. Usually, the 'short' period consists of no more than six months in industrial countries.

For some transition countries, Mills and Pentecost (2000) found different output responses in the period 1992–1998. A 1 per cent real devaluation led, after a delay of one quarter, to a monotonic, but slow rise of output of 1 per cent after approximately two years in Poland. For Slovakia, a 1 per cent real devaluation led to a 0.4 per cent fall in output just after one quarter. A real exchange rate change had no long-run effect on output in the Czech Republic, but accelerated output volatility. One of the explanations of non-standard responses in transition countries is quality. The Marshall–Lerner condition applies to cost-determined goods. Investors in transition countries needed advanced technologies in order to restructure companies and to improve the quality of exportable goods. Private households demanded, at least at the beginning of transition, Western products, which they assumed to have a higher utility than domestic products. A devaluation would certainly raise the price of imported goods, but elasticity of demand was weak, for investors as well as private households made their decisions with respect to quality and product variety.

With some longer period of weak price elasticity of import demand, the prevailing short-term effect of a depreciation would be rather the upsurge of inflation. In many transition countries, the costs in terms of an acceleration of inflation were higher than the weak quantitative responses of exports, import demand, and output. With this experience, governments withdrew from a policy of a competitive exchange rates. Later, most currencies appreciated in real terms and contributed to a deterioration of the trade balance (see the example of Poland in Figure 6.2). But this was already under the impact of the second problem: the strong inflow of partly undesired foreign exchange coupled with financial investment, which we will discuss on page 107.

Estimating the equilibrium exchange rate

The Marshall–Lerner condition states that if we want to improve net exports by using the exchange rate policy as a tool the sum of the exports and imports elasticities must be greater than one. This statement implies that only relatively slight changes of the exchange rate will be necessary to achieve a new trade equilibrium.

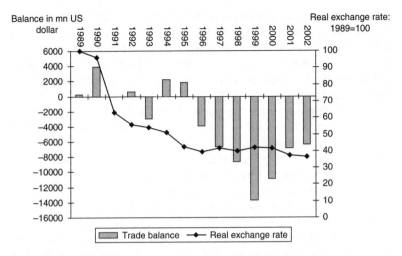

Figure 6.2 The real exchange rate of the Zloty and the trade balance of Poland[a] 1989–2002

Note: [a] Note that a fall of the real exchange rate index is a real appreciation!

Sources: Own calculations based on UN–ECE (2003) and IMF data.

In order to validate the above statement, the equilibrium exchange rate of the accession countries can be estimated with the aim of identifying, whether the exchange rate has a track record of overvaluation or undervaluation. For this purpose the concept of *fundamental equilibrium exchange rates (FEERs)* is used. This concept assumes that a balance in the economy has two dimensions. The first one is the *internal balance,* defined as the output consistent with both full employment and a low inflation rate. The second dimension is the *external balance,* characterised by a sustainable desired net flow of resources between countries when they are in internal balance. This approach abstracts from short-run cyclical conditions and temporary factors, as it relies on economic fundamentals, which are assumed to persist over the medium term. These conditions should be expected to ensure a sustainable balance in the economy. However, one should note that this method is rather a normative one, as the equilibrium exchange rate is based on the desirable economic conditions. The balance between demand and supply implies that there is no output gap and that savings and investments are sustainable. It does not, however, mean that *full stock flow equilibrium* is achieved.

Accession countries have experienced many shifts in exchange rate regimes since the beginning of the transition period. This substantially affects the results of trade elasticity estimations, which, in turn, influence the real exchange rate obtained. Parameters of the price elasticities have significant impact on the FEER estimations, as their value determines how much the real exchange rate has to alter to bring the economy into internal and external balance. The higher price elasticity is the smaller changes in real exchange rate required to correct disequilibrium.

The empirical findings are best illustrated by the case of Poland, which is chosen for its importance due to its size as well for its analytical interest due to being characterised above as being 'on the edge'.

Figure 6.3 compares the Polish real exchange rate (REER) with the FEER for Poland; it can be seen that only after the dramatic devaluation of 1992 is the Zloty below its FEER – i.e. undervalued. From 1995 onwards the real Zloty rate is above its FEER value, interrupted only by 2001–2, where it is in equilibrium due to a reduction of the trade deficit. The econometric analysis displays a long history of overvaluation of the Polish Zloty.

Figure 6.3 shows the degree of this overvaluation as the percentage difference between FEER and REER. It can be seen that the Zloty is still within the, Exchange Rate Mechanism (ERM)-II band of 15 per cent below or above the agreed parity. In our case, it can be assumed that the FEER reflects this parity. It does, however, move narrowly along this margin. With respect to economic policy it needs to be stressed that our econometric model does not capture portfolio choice on the market for foreign exchange. Obviously an exchange rate movement

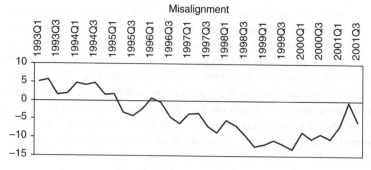

Figure 6.3   The overvaluation of the Zloty, 1993:1–2001:3

towards the lower margin could trigger a speculative attack. This vulnerability against monetary and financial crises was discussed in Chapter 5.

Capital account liberalization

Most economists agree that, after the experience of financial crises in South-East Asia and Latin America, capital controls should be lifted with much caution. Transition countries liberalized trade earlier, and more comprehensively, than the capital account, for they did not yet possess an adequate monetary order and financial sector (remember Chapter 3). Furthermore, they tried to avoid capital flight. Nevertheless, the problem of undesired capital flows and capital account liberalization began seriously in the mid-1990s, after initial political and economic stabilization. EU association countries opened their financial sectors to foreign capital when they became members of the OECD, and capital movement liberalization was almost completed at the time of EU entry. Non-EU candidates, however, retained important restrictions (Russia and other Central Asian successor states of the Soviet Union, and China).

What are undesired capital flows? NCFs include FDI, portfolio investment, and credits. No capital movement is necessarily a problem for a robust economy, when the capital inflow is of long-term character (FDI, for example) and entails productivity improvements in domestic production. However, economists are more sceptical about short-term capital flows and portfolio investment, where financial investors are not guided by a direct investment into productive capacities. Purely financial investments are at the lower end of a 'pecking order' of international capital flows and require an efficient financial sector which is able to transform capital inflows into domestic lending with an appropriate risk structure, and they require a exchange rate and monetary policy which is different to the situation with capital controls. Otherwise, the potential for a financial crisis would increase. A matter of concern is short-term borrowing by domestic banks, particularly when this lending is induced by high domestic interest rates, and when it leads to long-term credits to the company or private household sector.

Transition countries liberalized long-term FDI inflows earlier than other long-term forms (such as land purchases) and financial investments. Indeed, the inflow of FDI accelerated during transition, and helped to restructure the economy in terms of technology and managerial knowledge. Short-term capital flows remained restricted, and were liberalized in the mid-of 1990s. When the risk premium of investing in a transition economy started to fall, particularly in advanced reform countries and future EU members, short-term capital inflows gained momentum. The countries became the increasingly attractive destiny for part of the huge financial capital world-wide. They faced this with an increasing instability of their exchange rate arrangement and still weak financial sectors. All exchange rates came under appreciation pressure. The central banks were in difficulties defending the fixed peg of the nominal exchange rate. In some transition countries, financial crises broke out (the Czech Republic, May 1997; Russia, August 1998, for example). This contributed to a general move from fixed exchange rates to floating exchange rates or to currency boards. However, nominal exchange rates underwent a longer period of appreciation with increasing capital inflows, partly of a speculative character, and BTs deteriorated. Over the entire period, the BTs of all transition countries (except Russia and Ukraine) remained in a deficit, which to a certain extent reflected the excessive appreciation of the exchange rate.

The most undesired capital export is capital flight. Capital flight may be motivated by political uncertainty, but also may reflect the existence of residents who have acquired wealth in a questionable way (by spontaneous privatization, for example). Capital account controls are ineffective to prevent capital flight (see the example of Russia in Chapter 9), if the devaluation expectation is very high. In extreme cases, the legal tender of the transition country is not accepted as store of value or medium of exchange. Capital flight then takes the form of dollarizization/euroization or the use as money of other substitutes such as land, precious metals, or other scarce resources. In the latter case we speak of a *barter economy* rather than a monetary economy.

Appendix: trade opening and negative value added

Ronald I. McKinnon presented the basics of the trade-output model for transition countries (McKinnon 1991): assume that the value added of a single industry in a small member of the CEMEA empire would be

$$V_i = P_i Z_i - P_m M \tag{6A.1}$$

that is, gross value or output minus the cost of intermediate inputs; P_i and P_m are the domestic currency prices for the finished product and material input, respectively. Let t_i be the implicit tariff-protecting domestic production of the finished product. This can be a tariff or, with general prohibition to import, an administratively set higher price of the domestic product. We get the gap between the foreign and the domestic price level:

$$P_i = (1 + t_i)P_i^* \tag{6A.2}$$

We neglect the exchange rate problem, assuming that one unit of the domestic currency exchanges for one foreign. The implicit export tax t_m on material inputs would be

$$P_m^* = P_m(1 + t_m) \tag{6A.3}$$

By division and rearrangement, we get

$$\frac{P_i}{P_m} = (1 + t_i)(1 + t_m)\frac{P_i^*}{P_m^*} \tag{6A.4}$$

The product of the first two terms on the right hand side of (6A.4) is the coefficient of protection:

$$1 + r_i = (1 + t_i)(1 + t_m) \tag{6A.5}$$

The domestic value added at world prices would be

$$V_i^* = P_i^* Z_i - P_m^* M \tag{6A.6}$$

and, inserting (6A.2) and (6A.3), we get

$$V_i^* = \frac{P_i Z_i - (1 + t_m)(1 + t_i)P_m M}{(1 + t_i)} \tag{6A.7}$$

Even if we assume that the value added in domestic prices is positive, it can be negative in world market prices, when only t_m or t_i are sufficiently high. We have already seen that when the Soviet Union suddenly stopped supplying cheap energy in 1991–1992, the finished goods industries of the partner countries produced negative value added, for the cost of material inputs in terms of world market prices increased by t_m. At the same time, the move to free trade let the domestic price for the import substitute of the finished good fall to t_i. Because of the ability to adjust in a short time after the breakdown of the CMEA and after the lifting of all import protection, those industries with a negative value added simply collapsed.

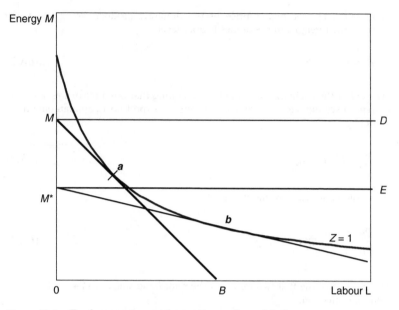

Figure 6A.1   Trade opening and negative value added

This model is shown in Figure 6A.1. Z is the output of a certain industry. We assume output to be 1. The indifference curve depicts all the combinations of labour and energy producing one unit of output. The initial situation in the closed economy is presented by the line BM, which has the slope P_i/P_m. With value added = 0, the point M represents output to be produced by energy only. Value added reaches its maximum at point a, for the relative price line of the closed economy is tangent to the indifference curve. This is a combination of artificial cheap energy with relatively expensive labour and protected output in the closed economy, achieved by SOEs and central planning. After the price increase in energy, a new price line emerges; point b reflects the optimal combination of inputs for one unit of output, with the new price line P^*_i/P^*_m. The value added is negative for all combinations above M^*. The difference can be calculated from (6A.1), (6A.5) and (6A.6) as

$$M - M^* = \frac{P_i}{P_m}\left(1 - \frac{1}{(1 + r_i)}\right) \tag{6A.8}$$

With a coefficient of protection of 0, $M = M^*$. The $DFMM^*$ area in Figure 6A.1 reports all points on the indifference curve where the combination of energy and labour yields a negative value added, the old situation of protection included. Opening trade requires restructuring, – that is, the replacement of expensive energy for cheaper labour. Such a restructuring requires investment and other efforts. In the meantime, output may collapse if no finance for restructuring is available.

Notes

1. For example, transfers resulting from workers employed abroad or gifts, etc.
2. We present industrial output rather than GDP, since industrial goods are the core of trade, while GDP includes also non-tradable services.

References and further reading

Akerlof, G.A., A. Rose, J. Yellen and H. Hessenius (1991) 'East Germany in from the cold: the economic aftermath of currency union', *Brookings Papers on Economic Activity*, 1.

Coorey, S., M. Mecagni and E. Offerdal (1996) 'Disinflation in transition economies: the role of relative price adjustment', IMF Working Paper 96/138).

Clark, P and R. MacDonald (1998) 'Exchange rates and economic fundamentals: a methodological comparison of BEERs and FEERs', IMF Working Paper 98/67.

Csaba, L. (1996) 'Hungary's trade policy between the Uruguay Round and EU accession', Kopint-Datorg, Discussion Papers 38, Budapest.

Eichengreen, B. and M. Mussa (1998) 'Capital account liberalization: theoretical and practical aspects', IMF Occasional Paper 172.

Gabrisch, H. (1995) 'Ostdeutschland und Mittel- und Osteuropa – ein vergleich der gesamtwirtschaftlichen Entwicklung', in R. Pohl (ed.), *Herausforderung Ostdeutschland: Fünf Jahre Währungs-, Wirtschafts- und Sozialunion* (Berlin: Analytica), 185–201.

Gácz, J. (1994) 'Trade policy in the Czech and Slovak Republics, Hungary and Poland in 1989–1993: a comparison', *CASE Studies and Analyses* No. 11.

Koen, V. and P. De Masi (1997) 'Prices in the transition: ten stylized facts', IMF Working Paper WP/97/158.

McKinnon, R. I., *The Order of Economic Liberalization: Financial Control in the Transition to a Market Economy* (Baltimore: The John Hopkins Press, 1991), Chapter 12.

Mills, T. C. and E. J. Pentecost (2000) 'The real exchange rate and the output response in four EU accession countries: business cycle volatility and economic growth', Research Paper 00–04, Loughborough University, Department of Economics; available at http://www.lboro.ac.uk/departments/ec/ Reasearchpapers/ BCV/bcv00–5/bcv00–5.pdf.

Organisation for Economic Co-operation and Development (OECD) (1996) *Purchasing Power Parities and Real Expenditures, Volume II* (Paris: OECD).

Richards, A. J. and G. H. R. Tersman (1996) 'Growth, nontradables, and price convergence in the Baltics', *Journal of Comparative Economics*, 23(2), 121–46.

Williamson, J. (ed.) (1994) *Estimating Equilibrium Exchange Rates* (Washington, DC: Institute for International Economics).

UN–ECE (1998, 2003, 2004) *Economic Survey of Europe* (New York and Geneva: United Nation Economic Commission for Europe).

7
Rising Income Inequality

A relatively even distribution of income was one of the classic attributes of the socialist system. This changed dramatically during the period of transformation but stabilized in CEE to almost continental European levels. Not so in Russia, where inequality levels remained significant. Chapter 7 is structured as follows. We first summarize the standard explanation for rising inequality, which is a microeconomic approach in a partial analytical framework. Its application to transition economies is briefly presented. We then reflect on the macroeconomic issues related to the distribution of income: various approaches are discussed in this context. We then present an empirical analysis of the Czech Republic, Hungary, Poland, and Russia, organized in a sequence of general income development, personal income distribution, and functional income distribution plus transfers. The following section reconsiders the performance of each country, and gives hypothetical explanations. The conclusion reviews the countries into the context of convergence and divergence.

Income distribution and convergence in the transition process[1]

Income distribution has dramatically changed during the transition from planned to market economies. The aim of this chapter is to clarify whether, and where, this statement is true, and how income distribution affects the overall growth performance of transition countries. There is a vast amount of literature on the real and nominal convergence of the 'new' EU member countries to 'old' EU member countries' standards,[2] but little is known about the behaviour of income distribution. Is the dramatic increase in income inequality overshooting EU levels or will there be a convergence in the sense of an assimilation to EU levels? The countries under review are: the Czech Republic, Hungary, Poland (as the most important new EU member economies) and Russia, in order to have a comparison with a non-EU accession country. The findings are analysed against the background of convergence or divergence, respectively, *vis-à-vis* the EU level of income and income distribution. Here Germany, being the neighbouring country and biggest EU economy, is taken as benchmark.[3]

The current state of the art in income inequality research can be summarized as the 'Transatlantic Consensus' (Atkinson 2000), which explains inequality through a partial analysis approach with changes on the labour market at its core. This approach, and its explanatory value for transition economies, will be critically discussed from a macroeconomic point of view. The potential interrelationship between inequality and growth is particularly important for transition countries because, according to conventional wisdom, these countries have experienced both rising inequality and declining GDP.

For the Czech Republic, Hungary, and Poland it can be shown that income distribution remained relatively stable before and throughout the transition period on the basis of so far unpublished data from the Luxembourg Income Study database. Russia, however, displays a sharp increase in inequality. These results are illustrated by Lorenz curves and underpinned by developments in functional income distribution.

The 'standard explanation' for rising inequality and its application to transition economies

The 'standard explanation' for rising income inequality relates income inequality to the labour market. According to this explanation, which Atkinson (2000) calls the 'Transatlantic Consensus', rising *wage inequality* is the key to conceptualizing rising income inequality in general. After a long period of lack of interest in the issue of income distribution, epitomised by Henry Aaron, who noted in 1978 (see Gottshalk and Smeeding 1997) that tracking changes in the distribution of income in the United States 'was like watching the grass grow' a new interest emerged. Since the early 1980s rising wage dispersion could be observed in the US labour market. Empirical studies show that these changes in earnings lead to rising inequality of household incomes. A similar observation could be made in the United Kingdom and continental Europe, although on the European mainland rising inequality went along with increasing unemployment.

The mechanics of the 'Transatlantic Consensus' are as follows: a shift in relative demand from unskilled to skilled workers leads to higher wages dispersion, because the wage premium increases in favour of those who are employed in the skilled labour sector. As wages for workers in the unskilled labour sectors fall, the overall inequality in earnings widens. The channel for this to the European continent (in particular, France) is that effective minimum wage protection leads to higher unemployment rather then decreasing wages for unskilled workers. Although there is widespread agreement on the mechanics of rising inequality, the reasons for the shift away from unskilled to skilled workers are disputed. *Globalization* and *technology changes* are most prominently featured and refer to the increase in international trade and the advent of electronic commerce. Whatever the reasons for the shift *per se* are, for the purpose of this analysis it seems noteworthy that the mechanics of this partial analytical 'standard explanation' are robust enough to create the 'Transatlantic Consensus'.

This analysis has been extended to the transition economies of Eastern Europe and further east by Milanović (2000), who has also written the most authoritative empirical overview so far (Milanović 1998). Milanović defines the transition from planned to market economies as 'the removal of legal restrictions on the private sector'.[4] For the pre-transition scenario it is assumed that the majority of workers were employed in the state sector and that income there was distributed more equally – albeit at a lower level – than in the private sector.[5] Within this set-up the same mechanics as in the 'Transatlantic Consensus' operate: parallel to the demand-shift story of western industrialized countries, a shift from state sector employment to private sector employment in the transition countries explains rising inequality in earnings and finally rising general inequality. Again, the robustness of the partial analytical approach is striking. We shall return to the explanatory power of the approach for the economics of transition after the consideration of the macroeconomic aspects of income distribution in the following section.

Macroeconomic aspects of income distribution

From a macroeconomic point of view, the labour market explanation for inequality can be only part of the story, because there are more sources of income than wages. In the tradition of David Ricardo a distinction needs to be made between *transfers* (rent in Ricardo's terminology), *profits* and *wages*. The focus of interest in macroeconomics is the functional distribution of income rather than the personal distribution. Traditionally functional income distribution is conjunct with 'laws' of economic development. For example, Ricardo created his hypothesis of the stagnation of capitalist development on the basis of his assumption that final production would be for the benefit of the rent recipient (the landlord) only. Ricardo's pupil Marx, however, concluded that the breakdown of capitalism would occur because the profit shares of income would increase so much that the exploited working class would overthrow the whole capitalist system. In modern approaches, rising inequality is limited by a *poverty line*, below which macroeconomic stability will be jeopardized by political unrest.

Kuznets' seminal work on the relationship of economic growth and income inequality asked the following question: 'Does inequality in the distribution of income increase or decrease in the course of a country's economic growth?' (Kuznets 1955, p. 1). Kuznets focused on long-run developments including sectoral changes from agricultural to industrial production and the emergence of services. His observations led to the so-called 'Kuznets curve'. The Kuznets curve has an inverted U-shape and its message is that rising inequality is growth-supporting initially, but after reaching a certain maximum of inequality, rising equality will be growth-supporting.

Compared to Kuznets, who always stressed, that 'distribution should be complete, i.e. should cover all units in a country' (1955, p. 1) the most obvious weakness of the labour market explanation of income inequality in the 'Transatlantic Consensus' is that it neglects unemployment to the extent that it cannot be explained by minimum wages. It also has little to say about non-voluntary unemployment. This is an important methodological limitation. Either the focus is the labour market, or it is not. There is little room for heterogeneity of labour beyond skilled and unskilled. A macroeconomic approach would look at the aggregate demand for labour and its effect on labour markets and income creation. At the end of the chain one would expect some effect on income equality, which might indeed to a certain extent be related to changes in earnings – i.e. the labour market – but would take further sources into account.

The macroeconomic approach would also have to emphasize that a demand-shift story within the labour market like the 'Transatlantic Consensus' suffers from any reaction of the stock of human capital. At least in the longer run, economic intuition would have to assume that workers would make an endeavour to move from the sector of unskilled labour into the sector of skilled labour by investment in education. This is a general macroeconomic aspect of the partial analysis which is particularly relevant for transition countries. In the rapidly changing environment for work during transition, 'old' human capital skills were devalued (much like the physical capital stock) (see for example Keane and Prasad 2000).

At the end of the twentieth century the general question of the interrelationship between the level of income per head/household and the distribution of income was a taken up again, this time by neoclassical growth theory. Barro (2000) provides evidence that higher inequality tends to retard growth in poor countries and encourage growth in wealthier countries. His broad panel of countries does, however, show little overall relation between income inequality and rates of growth and investment.

Transition economies are not included, as the period is presumably too short. The threshold between poor countries, where growth tends to fall with greater inequality, and rich countries, where growth rises with increasing inequality, is found 'around $2000 (1985 US dollars)' *per capita* GDP (Barro 2000, p. 32). This new approach to income distribution confirms the old view, because 'The Kuznets curve – whereby inequality first increases and later decreases in the process of economic development – emerges as a clear empirical regularity' (Barro 2000, p. 32).

Growth in transition appears to be a more complex phenomenon. Because the time span is relatively short, it is almost impossible to make a distinction between short-term and medium-term effects. Here, following Campos and Coricelli (2002), the term 'growth' refers to the short or medium term. The following section looks at what can be observed and whether or not Barro's statement above can apply to transition economies, too.

Some observations

This section presents empirical findings on general, personal, and functional (plus transfers) income dynamics and income distribution. Data on income distribution are obtained from the Luxembourg Income Study Database (LIS), which is considered to be global the most thoroughly validated dataset of household survey data. Data on functional income distribution plus transfers were obtained from the National Statistical Offices of the countries studied. The empirical approach differs from the Milanovic study quoted earlier as it is *income*-based rather than earnings-based, and this approach does provide a more complete picture of income distribution changes.

The Czech Republic, Hungary, Poland, and Russia were chosen because the first three countries are the economic 'heavyweights' in terms of GDP among the transition countries which recently joined the European Union. Russia is chosen as the 'heavyweight' of economic transition that does not have EU candidate status. A further pragmatic reason lies in the fact that relatively reliable data (although not always complete – see Russia, for example) in income distribution are available, which is not the case for South East European (SEE) countries and most of the former Soviet Union (FSU) countries.

General income development

As an introduction to income dynamics this sub-section looks at real GDP growth. Here we find a picture of convergence from and divergence to EU levels.

Figure 7.1 shows the development of real GDP in the Czech Republic, Hungary, Poland, and Russia measured with 1989 as the basis year. We find the so-called 'J-curve' of transformation in the case of Hungary and Poland, but a picture of recession and stagnation in the Czech Republic and long-lasting recession in Russia, which only latterly turned into considerable growth rates. For Hungary and Poland the J-curves show an upswing after the first years of 'transformation recession' and an economic recovery displaying higher levels of GDP in the longer run than before transition began. The Czech picture is characterized by stagnation after a short recovery from the early recession and even further recession after 1997, the year of the Czech banking and BOP crisis. The same year marks the lowest level of GDP in Russia, which coincided with the Rouble crisis. Interpretation of this graph has to be made with care, because the choice of the basis year is crucial and serious reservations about the comparability of data across the transition period are inappropriate. However, this method has been used by various institutions (including the World Bank, EBRD, etc.) and for the sake of comparability

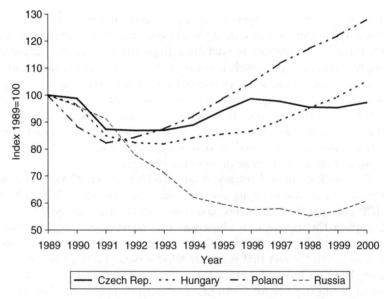

Figure 7.1   Development of real GDP during systemic transition, 1989–2000[a]

Note:

[a] It should be noted that this style of indexed presentation is chosen to compare the performance of the countries under review in this study. It does not say anything about the absolute level of income. Real GDP per head in the benchmark country, Germany, is 2–3 times higher.

with other studies the approach is maintained here. In this study the research question is how far this general economic performance can be related to the distribution of income.

Personal and functional income distributions

The analysis of personal income distribution is based on household surveys carried out by the authorities in the relevant countries validated by LIS.[6] *Household income* potentially includes every income source from the functional income distribution – i.e. a household might receive wages, profits, as well as transfers. Although the microcensus varies from country to country, they are validated by LIS to ensure comparability.

This analysis uses the *Gini coefficient* as empirical measure of income inequality. The Gini coefficient is derived from the cumulative distribution of earnings across the population as *per capita* incomes. It is defined as one-half of the mean difference between any two observations in the earnings distribution divided by average earnings. The higher the Gini coefficient, the higher is the inequality within a society. One familiar interpretation of the Gini coefficient is the *Lorenz curve*, which graphs cumulated income shares versus cumulative population shares. Population is ordered from low to high income. In this context, the Gini coefficient can be computed as twice the area between the 45° line that extends northeast from the origin and the Lorenz curve. The 45° line represents equal income distribution across the population and the larger the distance of the Lorenz curve to the equal distribution line the greater is income inequality.

The Lorenz curve for Germany in 1998 is taken as a benchmark. The reason for choosing Germany 1998 is first of all that it follows conventional research practice in using the former West Germany as benchmark for the former East Germany in almost any economic respect, including income distribution. More important is the fact that the former West Germany is regarded as a proxy for west European income distribution reflecting a social market economy expressed, *inter alia*, in an income distribution being much more equal than the United Kingdom but less equal than the Scandinavian countries.[7] The year 1989 is not problematic for Germany as in West Germany income equality was very stable over the years.

Tables 7A.1–7A.3 in the appendix (pp. 133–4) give more detailed information of what is illustrated and briefly discussed here by Lorenz curves. Table 7A.1 shows the cumulative personal income distribution of selected countries and years and in comparison to Germany 1998 (per household) in percentage cumulated quintile shares and the change *vis-à-vis* Germany as a benchmark. Table 7A.2 displays changes of personal income distribution of selected countries between selected years (per household) in percentage change rates in quintile shares. Table 7A.3 shows the distribution of household income according to decile shares (per household), in percentages.

A functional income distribution is presented here for two reasons: (1) to capture the macroeconomic aspects of income distribution and (2) to give a picture of the sources of incomes for the following discussion of personal income. The aim is also to provide evidence for an overall analysis of economic performance and the interrelationship between profits and investment. In addition, an attempt will be made to relate changes in personal income distribution to changes in functional income distribution, transfers, and other factors. As there are methodological problems in cross-country comparisons of profit ratios, etc., because of different national definitions and tax systems, the emphasis here is placed on change rather than absolute size, and no benchmark country is chosen.

The Czech Republic

The Lorenz curve for the Czech Republic (Figure 7.2) shows an increase in inequality from 1988 to 1992, which developed at the expense of the lower decile share, whereas the higher deciles remained more or less unchanged. This is also the year of intersection with the German Lorenz curve with the intersection point within the middle classes. This can be read as saying that the initial transition recession lead to a higher share of the poor than in the benchmark country, Germany, but a higher share of the rich deciles as a proportion of national income. This is supported by the picture to be discussed in the functional distribution, where the transition recession created rising shares of profits and declining wages (Figure 7.3). The third Lorenz curve of 1996 lies slightly below the benchmark, indicating that the income distribution is rather more unequal in the Czech Republic, but well within the range of its neighbouring country in the West. It is also notable that there was no sharp change in equality, but rather a moderate and gradual development.

In Figure 7.3. it should be noted that there is a statistical break in reporting by the Czech Statistical Office after 1991. 'Business and others' is replaced by 'operating surplus' and other categories were changed as well. Nevertheless it seems remarkable that the share of profits grew in the beginning of transition only to fall sharply in later years. The dramatic rise of the profit share in the crisis year of 1991 reflects the realisation of quasi-rents during the initial transition. The coincidence between sharply rising profit shares and a crisis in general income development is notable. The adjustment followed one year later, when profit shares

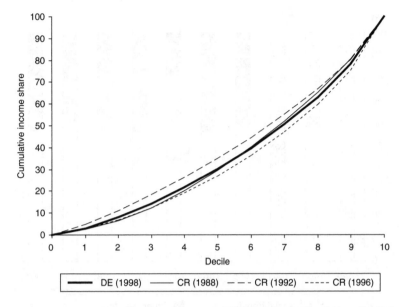

Figure 7.2 Personal income distribution, Czech Republic, 1988, 1992, and 1996

Note:
DE = Germany.
CR = Czech Republic.

fell as the consequence of falling investment in the previous year. Profit ratios (share of operating profits) increased slightly in 1993, but then remained stable until the 1997 crisis. The same observation holds for the wage ratios (labour compensation). Even property income shows only moderate changes. An increased share of profits went along with positive growth rates from 1994 to 1996. What is apparent is the stability of the functional income distribution over the transformation period.

Hungary

For Hungary, LIS has only two datasets, but again the message is clear. In socialist times the degree of inequality was nearly identical with the benchmark country, though at a far lower level. Inequality increased from 1991 to 1994, mainly to the benefit of the upper-middle classes, whereas the proportion of the lower deciles remained stable. As in the Czech Republic this move followed a rather modest and gradual path rather than displaying a dramatic jump in inequality (Figure 7.4).

For Hungary, the functional income distribution (Figure 7.5) also shows a jump in the profit share at the beginning of transformation, as

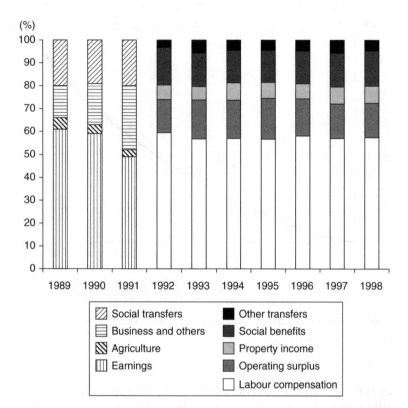

Figure 7.3 Functional income distribution and transfers, per cent of national income, Czech Republic, 1989–1998

in the Czech Republic albeit one year later (in 1992). An interesting detail is that property income doubled the year before and decreased to its normal level near 5 per cent the year after. It is surprising that this type of income was recorded in socialist times and we may suspect that property owners made a fortune in the initial year of transition. Social transfers plummeted after the end of communism, but the wage ratio rose above 60 per cent in the years 1992–1994. The proportion between wages and profits changed in 1995, the year of the austerity programme in Hungary. In that year the profit share grew to more than 20 per cent and remained on that level until today. Wages account for around 60 per cent. Social transfers were reduced as well, and remained around 10 per cent from 1996 onwards. Across the board, functional income distribution can be characterised as being stable. The comparison between personal income distribution and functional income distribution including

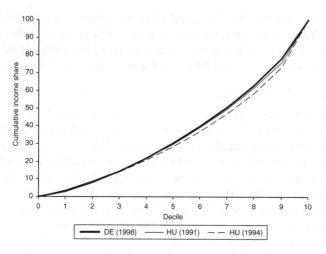

Figure 7.4 Personal income distribution, Hungary, 1991 and 1994

Note:
DE = Germany.
Hu = Hungary.

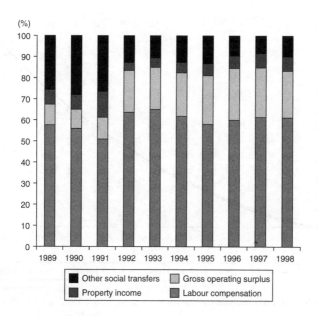

Figure 7.5 Functional income distribution and transfers, per cent of national income, Hungary, 1989–1998

transfers suggests, that the jump of profit quotas between 1991 and 1994 affected only the top decile, whereas the upper-middle classes lost income shares as shown in the wider distance of the 1994 Lorenz curve from the 45° line (see also Tables 7A.1 and 7A.2) in the Appendix.

Poland

A picture similar to Hungary has been found for Poland. Here there is only a very marginal increase in inequality until 1992, but a considerably higher degree of inequality in 1996 (Figure 7.6). It is notable that this increase developed for the benefit of the upper-middle classes, whereas the top decile and the lower deciles remained relatively stable. The degree of inequality is slightly below the benchmark. The overall picture is well in line with that of the Czech Republic and Hungary, representing a gradual move towards higher inequality, which is within the range of EU inequalities.

For Poland, at first glance the proportions of profits and wages seem to be unusual, but the size is influenced by the tax system and cross-country comparisons of the absolute size of quotas are not intended here (Figure 7.7). The focus of interest in this study is change rather than size.

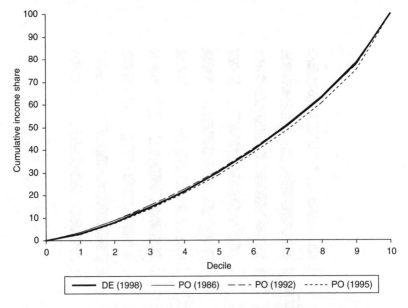

Figure 7.6   Personal income distribution, Poland, 1986, 1992, and 1995

Note:
DE = Germany.
PO = Poland.

In 1989 and 1990 earnings were not divided into wages and surplus. The first observation is that social transfers decrease in the initial phase of transformation and remain slightly above 10 per cent from 1993 onwards. One reason for this relative high level are pension payments, which were kept at levels very close to previous earnings of the recipients. Apart from this aspect, the functional income distribution remains stable throughout the transformation. The share of wages displays almost no change and profits sometimes increase slightly at the expense of property income and vice versa, but these minor movements are probably caused by interest rate variations. As interest payments are the major factor in property income, an increase in the market rate of interest increases this

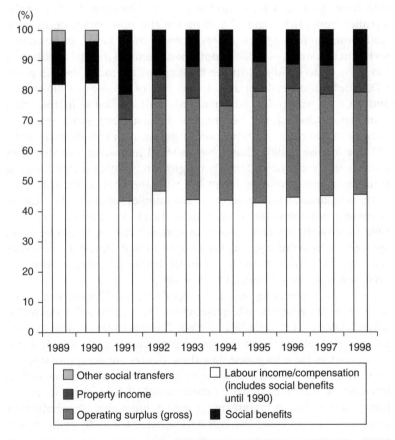

Figure 7.7 Functional income distribution and transfers, per cent of national income, Poland, 1991–1998

component of functional income distribution. Again, we find a picture of stability, if other sources do not grow correspondingly (*ceteris paribus*). Like Hungary, the jump in profits from 1992 to 1995 benefited the top decile only, but decreased the income shares of the upper-middle classes as shown in the widening distance of the 1995, curve in particular for the deciles 5–9 (see also Tables 7A.1 and7A.2) in the Appendix.

Russia

Russia is different. Even in communist times the level of inequality was higher than in other European socialist countries and it was also higher than in Germany. Secondly, there is a sharp increase in inequality from 1991/1992 to 1995/1996,[8] which went along with declining GDP. Thirdly, the winners are clearly the people in the top decile. There is a shift from the deciles 1–7 up to the top decile creating the class of the so-called 'super rich' Figure 7.8. However, this observation needs to be read more carefully against observations in the other countries under review in this study, as the development of personal income distribution has to be understood against the Russian background of declining real GDP. The bottom decile received 1.4 per cent of income (see Tables 7A.1 and 7A.2 in Appendix), which is only half the value in the other countries, including the benchmark. This suggests more extensive poverty in the course of transition in Russia. Also the distance to the 45° line for the middle classes has widened indicating a further shift towards the 'super rich'. These two aspects raise some methodological concerns about measuring inequality with the Gini coefficient. If we have, as in Russia, a hollowing out of the middle classes and the creation of poverty and a new class of 'super rich', then it does not seem very sensible to take the average income as denominator. It would be more appropriate to define a *poverty line* in order to find the real dimension of the tragedy in income inequality in Russia. For the sake of coherence, this exercise has not been pursued in this study.

For Russia, property income is not reported. Figure 7.9 shows a falling share of profits, which is no surprise against the background of Figure 7.1, where a falling GDP could be observed. The lack of investment leads to falling profit ratios, whereas wages remain more or less stable. It seems as if transfers have increased, but these figures are an approximation (against net taxes *ceteris paribus*) only, and care should be exercised in interpreting this data. With its continuously falling share of profits Russia stands out as a case of changing functional distribution of income. We may suspect that this development led to declining investment and, as a consequence, declining GDP.

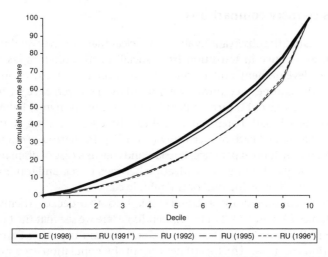

Figure 7.8   Personal income distribution, Russia, 1991, 1992, 1995, and 1996

Note:
DE = Germany.
RU = Russia.

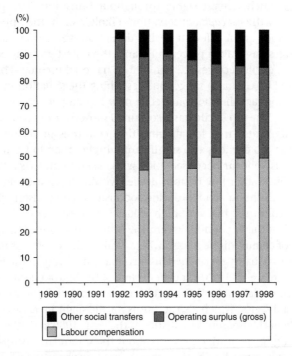

Figure 7.9   Functional income distribution and transfers, per cent of national income, Russia, 1992–1998

Cross-country comparisons

To summarize the observations above, it is clear that we have two different sets of experience in transition from socialism to capitalism, as far as income development and income distribution is concerned. At first glance, the European countries seem to follow a convergence path well within the range of EU income distribution, although slightly below the German benchmark Lorenz curve. All the three EU accession countries followed a gradual path of increasing inequality. In sharp contrast to the European transition experience, Russia stands out as a case of dramatically rising inequality leading to polarization between lower- and top-income classes and a 'hollowing out' of the middle classes.

This is confirmed by a closer look into the deciles themselves (see, Tables 7A.1 and 7A.2 in the Appendix). Here we see that the bottom decile in Russia is half of the size of Germany and the other European transition countries. The top 10 per cent of the population accumulates about one-third of national income in Russia, whereas this income class gains about one-fifth to one-quarter in the other countries. The European household statistics display strong middle classes in the European countries, which remain stable throughout transition. The picture is confirmed by the *per capita* observations (Table 7A.2 in the Appendix).

A closer look at the relevant deciles does, however, reveal that significant changes have taken place. In Poland, the fastest-growing economy, the bottom decile receives 2.7 per cent of national income. This is well within the EU (German) range. But describing the situation in this way overlooks the fact that bottom decile now has 25 per cent less income than before. The top decile has also gained most over the course of transition. This is also true for all transition countries under review. The share of the top decile is also significantly higher than in Germany.

There is also one further observation with regard to the Czech Republic.[9] Here, we find rather low bottom deciles within the household statistics (Table 7A.1 in the Appendix) during socialism in comparison with other transition countries, but very high values within the *per capita* statistics (Table 7A.2 in the Appendix). Vecernik (2000) has interpreted this as a consequence of communist ideology, where family values were less important compared to equality *per capita*. This has changed sharply in the transition period, where we find a 20 per cent decline of the bottom decile *per capita*. This can be explained by the fact that many women left the workforce of the low-paid sector, which also accounts for the slight increase of the bottom decile in the household statistics in the years 1988 and 1996.

Returning to the initial question about the interrelationship between growth and income distribution, the observations have to be interpreted

gang from 6.4 to 13.4 (see Schneider and Enste 2000, p. 101) in the Czech Republic. If we assume that profits are not declared, then higher-income categories have benefited most from moving into the black economy. Also the lowest category of incomes, which were characterized by a high number of children, might be part of the shadow economy, as this group consists largely of Roma families who tend to have more children but are not officially registered. The degree of correction of the Czech stability picture must be uncertain by nature of the argument.

Finally there seems to be some evidence for turning on its head the point made by Dollar and Kraay (2000), stating that 'growth is good for the poor', depending on the state of development in economies of transition. Taking Barro's $2000 threshold not seriously but as an illustration (Barro 2000), it could be that inequality is too low to allow for the emergence of the Kuznets curve. Not even Barro would go so far as to suggest an income distribution policy in favour of the rich, but the infrastructure for the creation of profit expectations in the official private sector might demand a potential for higher inequality in the Czech Republic (see Hölscher 2000a). The stability of social transfers shown above does not work in that direction and a diversion into education could be carefully advised. The argument is reinforced by rising unemployment in the Czech Republic. But, as stated earlier, the case for using the Kuznets curve for such a short period of time is problematic.

Hungary and Poland can be explained quickly, as here we find the situation where a rather high level of equality ensures the social acceptance of the reform process. We have located these two countries slightly before the maximum of the Kuznets curve. This implies that we have not yet reached the benchmark scenario of Germany, where it can be assumed the growth on a high level of income is supported by more equality within the society. Some more inequality for the benefit of the upper-middle classes (deciles 6–8) in Hungary and Poland would probably have a growth-promoting effect though increased demand for household consumption. In principle we have a 'well-behaved' Kuznets relationship between equality and growth in Hungary and Poland.

The Russian case raises the question of how this population managed to survive transformation without major civil wars or other forms of political unrest. What springs to mind in the first place is the huge non-market subsistence sector which kept households alive through *dacha* farming. Schneider and Enste (2000) estimate the size of the shadow economy in Russia at 20–27 per cent (higher values are estimated for other FSU countries). Secondly, the political system in Russia is apparently able to pacify society even although inequality is rising dramatically. Thirdly, Russia has experienced a longer period of declining income, following the J-curve pattern, which certainly had a strong impact on the lower-income classes and increasing poverty. Gradstein and Milanović (2002) suggest that democratic experience might play a crucial role in income inequality. Such a historical approach clearly points towards the difference between the CEEC, and Russia. The conclusion on economic policy will have to take experience from developing countries into account for the case of Russia.

Convergence versus divergence

This chapter shows that one must be careful in arguing that there is a causal relationship between general income creation, or even growth, and equality in terms of an interpretation of the direction has to be very careful. Income distribution seems to be a social variable that needs to be seen in its entire historical context. Even if the Kuznets curve can be observed as an empirical regularity, the explanation for this regularity remains dubious.

Progress, however, has been made in measurement and data collection. This is not always true for transition economies, where assessments sometimes very quickly become outdated by a turn of events. In this chapter, demystification of the J-curve of transformation as well as a Kuznets curve of transition in Eastern Europe are considered to be the major contribution to progress in economic knowledge.

This finally raises a question about the role of the state with regard to income equality in the transition process. The political economy of transition has pointed to political constraints (see, for example, Roland 2001) and the convergence in income distribution to German (or EU) levels is well documented and mirrored in, for example, the creation of convergence to EU levels of law and property rights. The interesting findings of this chapter are that for other issues of EU accession the new members have been set clear criteria – be it the Maastricht Treaty, the *acquis communitaire*, or ERM II – which in themselves might have set a convergence process towards EU standards into motion. Certainly incentives were created – which do not exist for Russia, which finds itself within an entirely different historical context, including a very different set of institutions of society and governance. Democracy as such is not a sufficient explanation, as while Russia's post-communist reforms were accompanied by huge increases in inequality, the reverse happened in Hungary, the Czech Republic, and Poland. To identify institutional factors in respect of income distribution more precisely, a more advanced research design is required. This raises a new conceptual challenge of the frameworks used to study growth and income distribution in the transition process.

Appendix: income statistics

Table 7A.1 Cumulated personal income distribution, selected countries and years, and in comparison to Germany, 1998 (per household), percentage cumulated quintile shares

	Lowest fifth		2nd fifth		3rd fifth		4th fifth	
	Cumulated income	Difference from Germany 1998	Cumulated income	Difference from Germany 1998	Cumulated income	Difference from Germany 1998	Cumulated income	Difference from Germany 1998
Czech Republic:								
1988	6.6	−1.4	20.1	−1.7	40.1	0.4	65.3	2.3
1992	11.2	3.2	26.4	4.6	44.6	4.9	66.8	3.8
1996	6.7	−1.3	19.0	−2.8	36.3	−3.4	59.9	−3.1
Hungary:								
1991	8.7	0.7	21.8	0.0	39.0	−0.7	61.5	−1.5
1994	8.1	0.1	20.7	−1.1	36.9	−2.8	58.4	−4.6
Poland:								
1986	8.7	0.7	22.1	0.3	40.1	0.4	63.7	0.7
1992	9.0	1.0	22.7	0.9	40.2	0.5	62.8	−0.2
1995	7.7	−0.3	20.9	−0.9	38.2	−1.5	60.6	−2.4
Russia:								
1991	7.7	−0.3	20.3	−1.5	37.2	−2.5	60.1	−2.9
1992	4.8	−3.2	13.7	−8.1	27.8	−11.9	49.1	−13.9
1995	4.5	−3.5	13.9	−7.9	27.8	−11.9	49.0	−14.0
1996	4.1	−3.9	13.1	−8.7	27.6	−12.1	46.0	−130

Notes: Data for differences to Germany 1998 are in percentage points with positive numbers indicating higher quintile shares as compared to Germany. The highest fifth equals 100 per cent.

Sources: LIS Database Sigmund (1998).

Table 7A.2 Changes in personal income distribution, selected countries, between selected years (per household), *percentage change rates*

	Lowest fifth	2nd fifth	3rd fifth	4th fifth
Czech Republic:				
1992/1988	69.7	31.3	11.2	2.3
1996/1992	−40.2	−28.0	−18.6	−10.3
Hungary:				
1994/1991	−6.9	−5.0	−5.4	−5.0
Poland:				
1992/1986	3.4	2.7	0.2	−1.4
1995/1992	−14.4	−7.9	−5.0	−3.5
Russia:				
1992/1991	−37.7	−32.5	−25.3	−18.3
1995/1992	−6.3	1.5	0.0	−0.2
1996/1995	−8.9	−5.8	−0.7	2.0

Sources: See Table 7A.1.

Table 7A.3 Distribution of household income according to decile shares (per household), *percentage decile shares*

Decile share	Czech Republic			Hungary		Poland			Russia				Germany
	1988**	1992	1996**	1991	1994	1986	1992	1995	1991*	1992	1995	1996*	1998***
1	2.5	4.9	2.8	3.5	3.1	3.6	3.7	2.7	3.1	1.8	1.4	1.4	2.8
2	4.1	6.3	3.9	5.2	5.0	5.1	5.3	5.0	4.6	3.0	3.1	2.7	5.2
3	5.9	7.2	5.6	6.1	5.9	6.1	6.4	6.1	5.8	3.9	4.2	3.9	6.4
4	7.6	8.0	6.7	7.0	6.7	7.3	7.3	7.1	6.8	5.0	5.2	5.1	7.4
5	9.3	8.7	7.9	8.0	7.6	8.4	8.2	8.1	7.9	6.3	6.3	6.5	8.4
6	10.7	9.5	9.4	9.2	8.6	9.6	9.3	9.2	9.0	7.8	7.6	8.0	9.5
7	12.0	10.5	10.9	10.4	10.0	11.0	10.5	10.4	10.5	9.5	9.3	9.9	10.8
8	13.2	11.7	12.7	12.1	11.5	12.6	12.1	12.0	12.4	11.8	11.9	12.5	12.5
9	15.1	13.4	15.4	14.4	15.0	14.9	14.6	14.4	15.3	15.4	16.7	16.9	15.1
10	19.6	19.9	24.7	24.0	26.6	21.4	22.5	24.9	24.6	35.3	34.2	33.1	21.9
1–10	100.0	100.0	100.0	100.0	100.0	100.0	100.0	100.0	100.0	100.0	100.0	100.0	100.0

Sources: See Table 7A.1.

Notes

1. Based on Hölscher (2006).
2. See Yigit and Kutan (2004) for an analytical review on the impact of European integration on convergence, using advanced comparison techniques.
3. Further reasons for the choice of this particular set of countries are given on p. 119.
4. The shortcomings of such an unusual definition of 'transition' will become evident later in the course of this chapter. At this stage, it is accepted for the sake of Milanović's argument.

5. We have some reservations concerning the empirical validity of this assumption, as there are pockets of very low wages in services industries in the private sector. For the sake of the model, however, this aspect is not pursued further here.
6. A previous version of this study was published in 2002 as Luxembourg Income Study Working Paper 275.
7. In the transition literature, the distance from Düsseldorf is used in a similar fashion as a proxy for distance from western European markets (see Campos and Coricelli 2002).
8. Data for 1991 and 1996 are obtained from Sigmund 1998 and refer to earnings rather than to income.
9. Unfortunately no coherent dataset was available for this country.
10. Some of the data presented in this study, in particular those on functional income distribution, rely on the yearbooks of the National Statistical Offices. Revised figures of previous years sometimes differ by almost 20 per cent. Another example is the paper by Keane and Prasad (2000), which rejects Milanović's findings on empirical grounds for Poland. These authors find similar results for Poland as this chapter does for the Czech Republic.

References and further reading

Aghion, P. and S. Commander (1999) 'On the dynamics of inequality in the transition', *Economics of Transition* 7(2).

Atkinson, A. B. (1999) 'Is rising inequality inevitable? A critique of the "Transatlantic Consensus" ', The United Nations University, WIDER *Annual Lectures* 3, Helsinki.

Atkinson, A. B. (2000) 'The changing distribution of income: evidence and explanations', *German Economic Review* 1(1).

Barro, R. J. (2000) 'Inequality and growth in a panel of countries'; available at www.economics.harvard.edu/faculty/barro/barro.html.

Campos, N. and F. Coricelli (2002) 'Growth in transition: what we know, what we don't, and what we should', *Journal of Economic Literature* 40, 793–836.

Dollar, D. and A. Kraay (2000) 'Growth is good for the poor' (Washington, DC: World Bank); available at, www.worldbank.org/research.

Gottschalk, P. and T. M. Smeeding (1997) 'Cross-national comparisons of earnings and income inequality', *Journal of Economic Literature* 35, 633–87.

Gradstein, M. and B. Milanović (2002) 'Does liberte = égalité?', Policy Research Working Paper 2875 (Washington, DC: World Bank).

Greenwood, J. and B. Jovanovic (1999) 'Financial development, growth, and the distribution of income', *Journal of Political Economy* 98(5).

Hölscher J. (2006) 'Income distribution and convergence in the transition process – a cross country comparison', *Comparative Economic Studies*, 48(2), 302–25.

Hölscher, J. (2000a) 'Income dynamics and stability in the transition process – general reflections applied to the Czech Republic', Center for European Integration Studies, University of Bonn, ZEI Working Paper B19/2000; available at www.zei.de.

Hölscher, J. (ed.) (2000b) *Financial Turbulence and Capital Markets in Transition Countries* (London and New York: Macmillan and St Martin's Press).

Honkkila, J. (2000) 'Inequality, restructuring and growth in transitional economies', Paper presented at the School of Slavonic and East European Studies, University College London.

Keane, M. P. and E. S. Prasad (2000) 'Inequality, transfers and growth: new evidence from the economic transition in Poland', IMF (International Monetary Fund) Working Papers.

Krelle, W. (1962) *Verteilungstheorie* (Wiesbaden: Gabler).

Kuznets, S. (1955) 'Economic growth and income inequality', *American Economic Review*, 45(1).

Luxemburg Income Study (LIS) Databank.

Milanović, B. (1998) 'Income, inequality and poverty during the transition from planned to market economy' (Washington, DC: World Bank).

Milanović, B. (2000) 'Explaining the increase in inequality during the transition'; available at www.worldbank.org/research/transition/pdf/employ2.pdf.

Roland, G. (2001) 'Ten years after ... transition and economics', IMF Staff Papers 48, 29–52.

Roland, G. (2002) 'The political economy of transition, *Journal of Economic Perspectives* 16(1), 29–50.

Schneider, F. and D. H. Enste (2000) 'Shadow economies: size, causes, and consequences', *Journal of Economic Literature* 38, 77–114.

Sigmund, P. (1998) 'Zur Lohn- und Einkommensentwicklung in Russland', Institut für Wirtschaftsforschung Halle, Forschungsreihe 5/1998.

Vecernik, J. (1999) 'Communist and transitory income distribution and social structure in the Czech Republic', The United Nation University, WIDER, Research for Action 51, Working Paper, Helsinki.

Vecernik, J. (2000) 'Distribution of household income in the Czech Republic 1988–1996: readjustment to the market', mimeo.

Vecernik, J. and P. Mateju (eds) (1999) *Ten Years of Rebuilding Capitalism: Czech Society after 1989* (Prague: Academia).

Yigit, T. M. and A. M. Kutan (2004) 'European integration, productivity growth and real convergence', Center for European Integration Studies, University of Bonn, ZEI Working Paper B08/2004; available at www.zei.de.

8
Transition and
EU Membership

Chapter 8 looks at the challenges for transformation concerning membership of the European Union. We concentrate on competition policy as the core of a competitive transformation and membership within the European Monetary Union (EMU) and its fiscal requirements. The chapter concludes with an exploration of fiscal transparency in the biggest new EU member country, Poland. We show that the EU law regarding competition policy has been implemented; the fulfilment of the Stability and Growth Pact (SGP), however, raises some concern, because the precondition of fiscal transparency cannot be taken for granted.

Competition policy[1]

Overview

Upon becoming a member of the European Union the new EU countries among other things had to adopt EU competition and anti-trust legislation. We need to take a closer look at this aspect, because we consider the competitive order of a market economy as a major challenge for transformation (see Chapter 4). The introduction of competition is the core challenge in the process of economic transition, as seen in our discussion of privatization and competition. One of the important questions concerning the latest European venture in eastward enlargement refers to the uncertainty of whether firms in the newly acceding countries will in fact be able to withstand intensified competition in the enlarged European market. There is a widespread concern among current members that the national governments of the accession candidates will revert to uncompetitive behaviour by unduly supporting their own industries. Apart from their typical labour cost advantage, it is feared that firms could benefit from unfair competitive advantages ranging from lower environmental standards and laxer merger control to price-distorting state aid. To ensure fair competition on a 'level playing field', the negotiations towards the final accession treaties feature an explicit consideration of such perceived problems. The objective of this chapter is to review the institutions and policies evolving in the field of competition in accession candidate countries: while a 'level playing field' can best be ensured by installing the same set of rules for policy and the same design of institutions, such an implantation of alien concepts might turn out to be incompatible with the general conditions prevailing on the markets of the country on the receiving end, in particular in the pre-accession period.

The general finding of this chapter is that great progress has been made in the course of accession negotiations with the European Union in respect to institution building and negotiations with the Union. The decision to join this club leads to a strong commitment to introduce and maintain competition. 2001 can even be seen as a landmark in negotiations on competition between the candidate countries and the Union as far as the adoption and enforcement of the Community's competition *acquis* is concerned. Negotiations with the Baltic States and Slovenia were largely concluded in 2002 (with the notable exception of agriculture and budgetary provisions) and further countries like Romania, Bulgaria and South East European countries are expected to follow soon. All accession countries have to implement the EU model of legislation, which itself is based on the German tradition of competition policy. The leading research question is therefore concerned with whether the adoption of the rule-based German model is in fact appropriate for the EU accession states. Specific circumstances of transition from communism to capitalism can generate particular problems of implementation, which require more measures than a simple takeover of EU rules. The peculiar circumstances of countries in transition are recognized by the Union, not least through the guiding negotiation principle of *differentiation*, which means that each candidate country is assessed as to whether or not it meets the EU requirements in its own right. This allows countries which began negotiations at a later stage to catch up and other countries to delay the transition process when it is thought necessary due to other policy objectives.

In general, the requirement of the agreement on competition policy is derived from the 1993 Copenhagen conference. In Copenhagen, the European Council decided on criteria to be met by applicants before joining the Union. In the economic sphere these criteria require the existence of a functioning market economy as well as the capacity to cope with competitive pressure and market forces within the Union.

With regard to competition policy, the Union has translated these criteria into three elements that must be in place in a candidate country before the competition negotiations can be completed:

(1) The necessary *legislative framework* with respect to anti-trust and state aid
(2) An adequate *administrative capacity* (in particular a well-functioning competition authority)
(3) A credible *enforcement record* of the *acquis* in all areas of competition policy.

We approach our subject by looking first at the EU–CEEC negotiation process itself. The selection of accession countries focuses on the group of most advanced, yet very differently structured, accession candidates – Slovenia, the Czech Republic, Hungary, and Poland. Romania serves this study as a comparison from the lower end of the transition progress spectrum. Having passed the first stage of accession negotiations, the Europe Agreements (EAs), the CEEs are now in the second stage of negotiations, which is concerned with the *acquis communautaire*. Where the relevant chapters on competition policy are still open, they are reviewed in detail in this section, in the context of the general economic environment of the chosen set of countries.

After this comprehensive overview we investigate the EU model of merger control and competition policy. Despite some obstacles partly because of the fact that EU anti-trust policy is undergoing a process of modernization itself, this model serves as blueprint for the implementation of competition policy in the new accession countries. We then review the implementation of the model in practice. Here, we look at legal transitions and provisions for competition policy and preliminary implementation experiences. These findings are illustrated by examples of merger control executed by the National Competition Offices. All anti-trust measures in the country sample between 1996 and 1999 are summarized and critically discussed. We conclude that competition policy in CEECs is well under way, although national differences persist.

Laws, regulations, and case law, as well as the institutions governing merger control as part of competition policy, had to be built from scratch in the CEECs. In the framework of the former economic regime with its close links between the state and the producing sector, competition policy was not only superfluous: the paradigm of economic planning stands in stark contrast to competition on markets. Additionally, in the case of some transition countries, institution building had to take place in a situation in which the state itself had been newly established – like the Baltic states, the Czech and Slovak Republics and the formerly Soviet and Yugoslav member states are examples. They could not benefit from past experiences within the borders of their new states and at least in the initial phase political concerns will have been of higher relevance. In this situation, transformation countries decided to go in different ways. The CEECs and Baltic countries decided for GATT and WTO membership and took the option of adopting the EU institutional set-up to short-cut the process of institution building with typical trial-and-error problems. Belarus, Russia, and Ukraine decided not to follow the way of at least becoming a WTO member, relying on a more 'independent' model of transformation (which often led into a cul de sac as in Belarus or Ukraine), fearing WTO rules of competition and liberalization which might mean that they could no longer make use of the comparative advantages of abundant energy and metals, and more or less subsidizing the use of these resources (forbidden for WTO members). Therefore, in these countries, the introduction of competition law (anti-trust, insolvency) was delayed (Russia) or never attempted (Belarus).

The EU–CEEC negotiation process

The EA: a first stage of negotiations on competition policy for CEECs

The Union itself justified this shortcut in the framework of the EA by offering the prospect of eventual EU accession following 'institution-copying' – in the case of non-fulfilment, the country's accession could be delayed or the country even excluded from membership. The EAs can be interpreted as creating a *de facto* rather than a *de jure* obligation for the CEECs to make internal competition law correspond to EU rules and to form the first of the two main stages of EU–CEEC negotiations with respect to competition policy.

The shortcut essentially comprised taking over a ready-made institutional system which had already stood the test of time and for which significant expertise in its implementation existed in case law. Apart from the preferential nature of this shortcut, it is however questionable whether the implementation of an alien system is in fact a feasible way to proceed: the EU system of competition policy had evolved from *harmonization*, and at a later stage by way of cooperation between mature market economies as a parallel system to national laws. It was essentially geared towards providing a counterbalance to the diminishing possibilities of intervention (e.g. protection of national industries by means of tariffs and exchange rates).

EU competition rules were not only designed with a view to economic efficiency but were implemented to prevent 'unfair competition' from foreign countries (e.g. safeguard and anti-dumping duties). What transition economies needed rather was a system more geared towards the promotion of *contestable markets* within their own economies – i.e. bankruptcy, corporate, and competition laws, as well as universally accepted accounting standards. This was not the main focus of the EU competition policy institutions.

EU competition policy – and in particular regulations referring to state aids – are also biased towards providing a 'level playing field' within industries across economies rather than between the variety of industries over the whole integration region. A system geared towards objectives of (EU-wide harmonized) industrial policy could prove to be disadvantageous in the case of transition economies: here, the initial task was to reform the vast structural distortions inherited from the socialist era of economic planning with its distinct industrial biases – i.e. to improve efficiency in the allocation of resources. Moreover, the industry-selective feature of EU state-aid regulations might even deter an accession candidate 'from promoting investment in areas where it had a genuine comparative advantage but where this might replace capacity existing elsewhere in Europe'. Some observers came to the conclusion that the implantation of the EU institutional framework for competition policy in transition economies was not really preferable, while others assess the net effect relative to the likely feasible alternative of institution building within the countries more positively.

In May 1995, the EU Commission expressed its views on the requirements of CEECs in terms of competition policy in a White Paper. In general, this stated more precisely the provisions as set out in the EAs, and expressed the view that the EAs obliged accession candidates broadly to adopt EU competition rules.

The second stage of negotiations: the *acquis* communautaire

A second stage of EU–CEEC negotiation process commenced when accession negotiations began. Until then, there had been no *de jure* obligation to copy EU competition policy (disregarding the opinion of the Commission expressed in the White Paper) and there was no time-frame for the adoption of rules. Since accession negotiations, however, CEECs are required to take over the *acquis communautaire* completely and within a defined period of time; the competition policy rules form part of this.

The EU legislative provisions are subdivided into thirty chapters covering political areas such as the 'common foreign and security policy', legal issues such as 'justice and home affairs', cultural issues such as 'culture and audio-visual policy' and a whole variety of economic issues ranging from the 'four freedoms' (force movement of goods, services, persons and capital) in the Single Market to 'environment' and 'competition policy'. Negotiations between the Union and accession states are organized under these chapters.

By October 2002, negotiations on all chapters have been opened, and most chapters have already been closed, at least provisionally. Our chapters of concern here – 6, 'competition policy' (formerly 14, 'competition and state aids'), and 15, 'industrial policy' had been opened for negotiations in all countries in our analysis under the German EU Council Presidency at a ministerial level. Chapter 6 was provisionally concluded with Slovenia in November 2001, in Hungary and Poland only in December 2002. Romania still remains in negotiations over the competition field. Chapter 15 on industrial policy has been closed in all the countries of our panel. There have been particular problems in the competition field. Table 8.1 provides an overview of the number of chapters concluded and the dates of opening and conclusion of negotiations on the chapters which have some bearing on competition policy.

This provisional closure of chapters does, however, not mean that a workable compromise for all issues in the chapter had already been found. It meant only that the majority of issues had been settled while some minor points, albeit particularly sensitive, ones were still unsettled (typically, this concerned the granting of derogations strictly limited in time). Chapters can therefore be reopened again by both sides at any time. The fact that even the chapter on 'industrial policy', the properties of which are closest to those of 'competition policy', has been closed in all accession countries underlines the provisional character of the negotiations. Furthermore, the formal closure of negotiations in any chapter should be regarded not only as provisional but also as confined to what both sides may have agreed upon in terms of regulations and rules. No immediate repercussions on national law or even the handling of respective topics at national levels can necessarily be expected from the closure of chapters as such. These need further approval by national legislative bodies with a view to implementation and adaptation.[2] Apart from this, those negotiations are a supranational political process and both sides have a rational motivation to keep chapters open: when concluding negotiations, compromises will be made not only within chapters but also between chapters.[3]

Table 8.1 EU accession negotiations: numbers of provisionally closed chapters and dates[a]

Chapters/Candidates	Hungary	Poland	Romania	Slovenia
Number of provisionally closed chapters	30	30	15	30
Years of opening/provisional closure of chapters:				
1 Free movement of goods	99–01[b]	99–01	02–	99–01
2 Free movement of persons	00–01	00–01	02–	00–01
3 Freedom to provide services	99–01	99–00	–	99–00
4 Free movement of capital	99–01	99–02	01–	99–01
5 Company law	98–01	98–01	01–01	98–00
6 Competition policy	99–02	99–02	00–	99–01
7 Agriculture	00–02	00–02	02–	00–02
8 Fisheries	99–99	99–02	01–01	99–99
15 Industrial policy	98–99	98–99	02–02	98–99
16 SMEs	98–98	98–98	00–00	98–98
19 Telecommunications and information technologies	98–00	98–99	00–02	98–99
21 Regional policy and coordination of structural instruments	00–02	00–02	02–	00–02

Notes:
[a] Situation as of the Copenhagen Summit of 12–13 December 2002.
[b] For ease of reading, the dates of opening and closure of chapters have been abbreviated.

Source: EurActiv.com Portal.

EU anti-trust modernization and competition policy

Legislation in the area of competition policy at the EU level takes the German or in the wider senses 'continental' tradition as its orientation. The general implication of this approach is that anti-trust policy in Europe is rule-oriented rather than relying on the case-by-case approach, which we can find in the Anglo-Saxon tradition of law. In terms of institutional design the EU-level competition policy is allocated to the Commission. We shall discuss aspects of this structure before the aspects of EU anti-trust modernization and its relevance for the accession countries are considered.

The German system has two authorities, the cartel office and the monopoly commission, acting on the basis of the 'Law against Limitations of Competition'. This law was implemented in 1957 and was created within the context of *'Ordnungspolitik'*, an influential Freiburg school of economic thought. The founding father of this way of thought was Walter Eucken, who laid the foundations in his work *Grundsätze der Wirtschaftspolitik* (Principles of Economic Policy, 1952).

The immediate consequence of the EU (German) model of rule-based competition policy is *external openness* for foreign trade and *internal price liberalization*. The case of transition economies illustrates that these two components are not enough to ensure competition, because there is an economic structure dominated by huge state monopolies from the communist past. This aspect is transition-specific and means that time for institution building and restructuring is needed for the creation of a competitive market order.

The EU (German) law is taken as blueprint and introduced with some modifications in transition countries. This law is normally structured as follows:

(1) General regulations
(2) Ban on collusion and collusive behaviour
(3) Procedures for exceptions
(4) Market-dominating enterprises
(5) Enterprises with special and exclusive rights or natural monopolies
(6) State aids
(7) Merger control
(8) Unfair competition
(9) State supervision authorities
(10) Responsibilities in case of violations of the competition law
(11) Application regulations.

This law has been implemented, with some country-specific modifications, across more or less all the transition countries which are EU membership candidates. There are, however, some important aspects to be considered. We focus on three economically oriented levels:

(1) Definition of the *relevant market*
(2) *Exemptions* from the rules
(3) *Modernization* of EU anti-trust law.

First of all, the definition of the *relevant market* in order to determine 'market domination' distinguishes between 'product' and 'geographical' markets. With respect to the latter, in many transition countries the relevant market is not the domestic market but the EU market as a whole. This is particularly important in the case of mergers and takeovers through FDI. National legislation falls short in regulating industry structure, and with the advent of globalization there are cases, where the 'relevant market' is the world market. With no global anti-trust authority in place this involves massive legal problems of regulation. In general, we can say that the definition of the relevant market has to go beyond national borders, the smaller the domestic markets are. This depends on the specific industrial structure but, *ceteris paribus*, a small economy (measured in GDP) will face a greater demand and subsequent opportunities for economies of scale beyond their borders. For transition countries, this aspect is of particular importance since all of them are small economies measured by GDP, the Baltics and Slovenia in particular. This problem is normally addressed through the possibility of *exemptions* from the law justified by the government or the anti-trust authorities, which leads to the second aspect noted above. In some cases domestic markets are so small that a market-dominating position of one enterprise is accepted for the sake of being competitive at the international level. This also depends on the traditions by which nations treat their national champions, a relevant factor for transition countries where state and public sector are still closely interrelated. In the original blueprint of the German Law the Ministry of Economics has within limits the right to allow market-dominating positions of enterprises and can overrule the decision of the anti-trust administration.

Also exempted from the ban on cartels are horizontal cartels, if collusion effects a market share of not more than 5 per cent (and vertical cartels with the same percentage). The criterion of a market-dominating position is a market share of 40 per cent[4] and identifiable independent behaviour of the enterprise in question. The same benchmark applies for enterprise alliances and mergers. In conjunction with competition policy, consumer protection is one aim of preventing unfair practices. This includes licensing for certain economic activities (such as trade in weapons, drugs, etc.) and qualification requirements to pursue certain professions (such as driving instructors, estate agents, doctors, etc.).

In practice, the application of the law in the transition economies is more complex. Here it should be noted that in nearly all transition countries, former state monopolies in power and energy, telecommunication, and water supplies exceed a market share of 40 per cent and deregulation is required to move towards a quasi-EU-type system. Deregulation by privatization is seen a one possible way out of the dilemma between the model and the practice of competition policy in transition countries.

The accession countries took over the EU model in a time when this model had came under growing debate within the Union itself. The modernization of EU anti-trust enforcement law through decentralization has now even become a paradigm for other decentralization activities. This means that the accession countries are joining the Union at a time when national competition authorities (NCAs) are likely to be given a more important role to play in competition policy. The elimination of the European Commission's exemption monopoly will have direct repercussions on the NCAs. The White Paper lacks some detail on the specific regulations envisaged, but clearly outlines principles of cooperation of a network of enforcement agencies: while EU law assumes supremacy over national law, NCAs are not obliged to submit cases of supranational interest to the Commission. The Commission, however, retains the right to intervene at its own discretion. This might confront accession countries with two sets of problems: the first is mainly related to administrative problems, least in the short run. For example, the notification system in some of the accession countries cannot be assumed as being equally efficient as in the Union. There might also still be some kind of 'stamp of approval culture' in place. The second problem is related to decentralization efforts: if NCAs in accession states still have a long way to go in terms of expertise and are supplied with an alien model, then active EU involvement in supranational competition disputes could in fact assist institution building and learning. In general, the progress of the negotiations suggest that the modernization of EU anti-trust law should not be a major obstacle for the enlargement process, although its implementation might be very difficult in practice.

This underpins the actual development in Europe, as it is envisaged to continue in the EU enlargement process. Liberalization of markets goes along with the creation of an EU-wide competition policy,[5] which in the near future might be enforced by national authorities. In comparison with the EU advancements, multilateral competition policy on a global scale within the framework of GATT WTO is still in its infancy and concentrates on price and cost dumping only. The OECD has agreed on some regulations in consultation between member countries in cases where interests of third parties are involved, but has not agreed on a set of binding rules. The United Nations Conference on Trade and Development (UNCTAD) has agreed on a 'Set of Multilaterally Agreed Equitable Principles for the Control of Restrictive Business Practises', which are binding, but very vague. On the global level the discrepancy between the model and the reality of competition policy is in even sharper contrast than in transition countries.

Conclusions

The analysis of EU–CEEC negotiation processes and anti-trust practice in CEECs suggests that competition policy in the accession states is well under way, and there appears to be no concern that merger control, in particular, is too lax. This even applies to Romania, despite the fact that systemic transition in this country is still young and institution building in general less developed as compared to the more advanced accession states under review. Those latter countries have by now implemented all the legislation pertaining to competition policy by taking over the relevant chapters from the *acquis communautaire*.

EMU membership

The East European enlargement process reached its final phase for a first group of countries, which joined the European Union on 1 May 2004. Upon accession, these countries became members of EMU with the transitory status of 'countries with a derogation'. Their central banks will become part of the European System of Central Banks (ESCB) and once they have achieved a certain degree of convergence, assessed on the basis of the Maastricht criteria, they will adopt the Euro and the central banks will become integrated into the Eurosystem. An interim phase of a two-year-period of participation in the European Exchange Rate Mechanism II (ERM II) type of arrangement is required. Its features are summarized in Box 8.1.

Given this 'one-size-fits-all' approach, it seems surprising that the entry strategies among the accession countries differ widely, from currency boards to free float, and even a serious consideration of unilateral Euroisation. It is noteworthy that even a currency board arrangement is possible in agreement with the ECB within ERM-II, which leaves only a free-float exchange rate arrangement and unilateral Euroisation as exchange rate arrangements directly violating the system. The range of exchange rate and monetary policy is summarized in Box 8.2.

All the policies sketched above are entry strategies for ERM-II. Despite the fact that they differ widely, the general observation is that these policies aimed to contribute strongly to the achievements in macroeconomic

---

Box 8.1   The components of ERM-II

- Precondition for participation in Euroland
- Fixed parity to the Euro (floating within a band up to +/– 15 per cent)
- Unlimited marginal interventions 'pre-paid' by national central bank concerned and financed by the ECB
- Intramarginal interventions can be financed by the ECB to a limited extent
- Confidential assessment of central parity.

Box 8.2 Exchange rates and monetary policies in the accession countries

Exchange rate	Monetary policy	Policy variable	Country
Currency board	exchange rate targeting (hard peg)	None	Lithuania Estonia Latvia Bulgaria
Peg +managed float	income targeting (+shadowing ERM II)	i, P, e	Hungary
Managed float	inflation targeting (+Euro as informal reference)	P	Czech Republic Romania[a] Slovenia[b] Slovakia
Free float	Direct inflation targeting	P	Poland

Notes:
[a] With capital controls.
[b] Uses monetary targeting as policy.
i = rate of interest; P = price level; e = exchange rate

Box 8.3 The Maastricht criteria

The Maastricht criteria, which are assumed to sustain the European Union in the future, specify in two separate Protocols five *convergence criteria* by which a country may be admitted:

- An inflation rate no more than 1.5 percentage points above the average of the three countries with the lowest inflation rates
- Nominal long-term interest rates not exceeding by more than 2 percentage points those for the three countries with the lowest inflation rates
- No exchange rate realignment for at least two years
- A government budget deficit not in excess of 3 per cent of each country's GDP
- A gross debt: GDP ratio that does not exceed 60 per cent.

stability. The current discussion in this area centres around the question of the optimal conversion rate *vis-à-vis* the Euro and how best to prepare for its adoption; Slovenia, Estonia, and Lithuania became members of ERM II in July 2004.

All EU members, including the newcomers, are obliged to conform to the Maastricht criteria laid down in the SGP (see Box 8.3).

The first three convergence criteria are designed to ensure monetary stability by supporting a fixed exchange rate regime among member countries. The stability of the Euro is reinforced by the last two criteria, which protect the Union from threats of inflation which may arise from government budget deficits. In this context, the first challenge for the transformation countries was to restore *fiscal transparency*.

Fiscal transparency[6]

The precondition in order to fulfil these criteria is the awareness of the state budget. The modern discussion centres around the issue of *fiscal transparency*. Transparency and fiscal rules can be of great help in reducing the deficit bias, and the importance of fiscal transparency is highly appreciated by such international organizations as the IMF, which has published *Codes of Good Practices on Fiscal Transparency* (1998), and the OECD, with its *Best Practices for Budget Transparency* (2000). Such rules have also been explicitly formulated by the European Union in the *acquis communautaire*. All these organizations emphasize the role of fiscal transparency as a precondition for fiscal sustainability and good governance and transparency is commonly supplemented by fiscal rules that are implemented to inject or restore credibility. They have been introduced as binding constraints by the Union in the form of the Maastricht criteria and the SGP. However, in order to fully benefit from such rules, fiscal policy has to be transparent, as this obliges policy-makers to become more accountable.

The issue of fiscal transparency has been examined theoretically in the literature. The central conclusion appears to be that the higher the degree of transparency, the higher the potential benefits in terms of greater fiscal discipline and more accountable fiscal policy. Other benefits are related to reduction of uncertainty in fiscal policy and faster and smoother fiscal policy responses to shocks hitting the economy. Empirical research confirms the positive impact of transparency on fiscal performance.

Transparency can be a powerful supplementary tool when setting, and subsequently executing, fiscal rules that are primarily introduced to gain credibility. This is particularly important for countries that seek to inject or restore credibility when initializing a reform package or following a crisis. An optimal solution to adopting fiscal rules seems to be a cyclically adjusted deficit alongside a debt ceiling and path that would be accompanied by a ceiling for expenditures. Empirical results tend to favour fiscal rules; however, in order to fully benefit from such rules fiscal policy has to be transparent, as this imposes pressure on policy-makers to be accountable. The issue of accountability can act as an important tool for politicians in pursuing a disciplined fiscal policy.

Fiscal transparency and rules in Poland

First, inflation led to improvement of the budget balance, for firms earned from inflation and tax revenues improved, despite severe output losses in the economy. Tax collection was weak and prevented a balanced budget despite high output growth. During the 1990s the central government deficit was reduced from 6.5 per cent of GDP (1991–1992) to about 3 per cent of GDP between 1993 and 1996 and to 2 per cent of GDP subsequently. Public debt was also reduced, from about 90 per cent of GDP in 1990.[7] In the first years of the transition the Paris and London Clubs of creditors agreed to write off a significant part of Poland's foreign debt. This operation also resulted in Poland regaining the credit capacity it had lost at the end of the 1970s, when the communist government refused to service its excessive debt.

Poland's fiscal policy stance started to deteriorate in 1999. The general government deficit increased to 3 per cent of GDP, despite a decrease in the central government deficit due to growing lending by off-budget institutions. This took place after the implementation of four key reforms of public sector institutions (the pension system, health service, local administration, and education). Low economic growth between 2001 and 2002 resulted in a further deterioration in the fiscal position. In the pre-accession period, Poland was also one of the CEECs to relax its fiscal policy. Between 2000 and 2004 the general government deficit increased from 3.0 per cent to 6.3 per cent of GDP. This was accompanied by a drop in privatization revenues, which tend to be used as an alternative to Treasury securities as a means of covering public sector borrowing requirements. This caused a significant acceleration of public debt from 2002 onwards. In 2003, public debt exceed the first threshold laid out in the Act on Public Finances (a debt : GDP ratio of 50 per cent), and in 2004 stabilized slightly below the second threshold (debt : GDP 55 per cent).

At the beginning of the 1990s Poland underwent significant structural reforms with the implementation of market economic rules. This was manifested in the acceleration of economic restructuring and a significant decrease in employment, among other things. The social costs of these reforms were partially offset by easy access to a wide range of social transfers. This, combined with widening indexation of budget spending, resulted in a significant increase in the Polish budget deficit. Economic slowdown, which began in 2000, revealed the structural problems inherent in Poland's public finances. It should also be noted that the reforms of the Polish public sector were significantly delayed compared to the wider economic restructuring process. Thus, the poor condition of public institutions in fact reinforced the underlying problems of the Polish budget in the years of economic slowdown. In 1999, the Polish government implemented key public sector reforms, but this added to the deteriorating condition of the country's public finance through their high initial cost. The positive aspects will be visible only in the longer term (for example, reforms of the pension system)

Political constraints also reduced the possibility of implementing radical spending reforms in subsequent annual budgets. In 2004, the government came up with the so-called 'Hausner [austerity] plan', but Parliament watered down much of its expenditure-cutting legislation, thus reducing any of the positive financial results that might have arisen from it.

The macroeconomic environment has also had a strong impact on fiscal performance, with the pace of economic growth and level of inflation determining the tax base and thus, in turn, general government revenues. Due to the cyclical character of revenues the flexibility of expenditures is necessary to maintain the budget deficit at a sustainable level even in years of economic slowdown. The significant share of fixed expenditures in Poland's central budget further reinforced the deterioration in the fiscal position between 2001–2002.

In both pre- and post-accession periods Poland failed significantly to tighten its fiscal policy. In 2004, Poland was one of six new member countries exceeding the SGP limit for the general government deficit. The first year of EU membership, which imposed an external anchor on the fiscal policies of the new member countries, appears not to have been an effective stimulus to fiscal tightening, so far at least. The lack of fiscal consolidation can partially be attributed to the high cost of accession. Estimates say that unless the new accession countries undertake major fiscal reforms the average direct budgetary cost of EU entry will widen the budget deficit by 3–4.75 per cent of GDP. Furthermore, the stronger bargaining position of the new member countries may be seen as an incentive to deviate from convergence towards the Maastricht criteria. As an additional factor explaining Poland's low propensity to tighten its fiscal stance after accession one can also note the dilution of sanctions for failures to converge to the deficit reference values. This was combined with a decrease in the role played by the SGP after unsuccessful attempts to impose economic sanctions on those EU member countries whose general government deficits were above the SGP threshold.

In the 1990s Poland experienced considerable improvement in its fiscal transparency. Two important developments bringing the conduct of policy closer to international standards of transparency were the implementation of a modern budgeting process and clarifying the boundaries of the public sector. Since 1998 fiscal management has been based on the Act on Public Finances, which comprehensively defines the responsibilities and activities of the government. Implementation of the Act enforces codified budgets and a far more stringent reporting process. It defines the use of budgetary reserves and provides for the imposition of sanctions for non-compliance. Finally, the Act classifies all public sector units and outlines financial management standards, as well as setting out a clarification of borrowing authority.

The reforms undertaken in the 1990s by other transition countries in the region were more advanced. This placed the conduct of Poland's fiscal policy far behind the transparent practices of most of the other new EU members. Considerable improvement in terms of transparency practices were made in the pre-accession period because of the obligation to create accountability standards as a condition for obtaining EU funds, as well as the implementation of more effective management to meet fiscal goals.

The following assessment of fiscal transparency is based on the questionnaire proposed by Allan and Parry (2003). The questionnaire was constructed by modifying the IMF's observance standards in order to highlight four areas that have particular significance for EU accession countries: (1) establishing a medium-term budget framework (MTBF); (2) comprehensive coverage of non-budgetary activities; (3) effective accounting, reporting, and oversight; and (4) strengthening intergovernmental relations. The authors also added point (5), which is concerned with audit functions and the Ministry of Finance's (MoF's) role and powers in the budgetary process.

As for transparency monitoring, one should note that Poland still has a deficiency in its budgeting process. This differentiates it significantly from the standards of an efficient MTBF. One of the most important weaknesses of Polish budgeting process is the *yearly outlook* of its planning. This is contrary to IMF recommendations, which propose the use of a medium-term framework or fiscal strategy to guide annual budget submissions. A yearly outlook does not allow any effectively links to be made nor credible budgeting planning with medium-term fiscal policy goals – connected, for example, with EU obligations. Budget planning should also be strictly based on medium-term macroeconomic projections. This makes decision-makers aware of revenue shortages connected with the economic cycle and thus allows them to control unrealistic budget bids. Poland's budgeting process is based on macroeconomic projections, but since they cover only a single year this makes any proper evaluation of medium-term macroeconomic risk (connected, for example, with cyclical fluctuation of output) difficult. Both the lack of long-term fiscal objectives in the yearly budget and the insufficient impact of medium-term macroeconomic estimates on the budget would suggest that the budgeting process in Poland is still more affected by short-term policy aims than medium-term objectives (for example, fiscal targets connected with accession to the EMU). The Budget Act outlines medium-term goals only in general terms. The Polish budgeting process also does not meet another feature of the MTBF, since it fails to make distinctions between *new* and *ongoing* policy costs. This undermines the establishment of accountability standards. On the positive side, there has been an increase in budgetary realism in recent years and fiscal sustainability and long-term risk analysis has been periodically performed.

In the second area of transparency monitoring – i.e. effective accounting, reporting, and oversight – Poland's performance continues to improve. The fragmentation of the Polish public sector is still significant, although in recent years considerable attempts to consolidate the sector have been undertaken. A few state agencies have been liquidated and other state offices consolidated into the government. Moreover, since 2004 a significant share of special funds have been included in the central budget. The MoF has started to move from a cash-based accounting classification (GFSM–1996) to an accrual-based system (GFSM–2001). The GFSM–2001 system is consistent with the ESA–95 format, which became the main fiscal indicator after accession.

In the third area of fiscal transparency – i.e. comprehensive coverage of non-budgetary activities – Poland has seen a noticeable improvement. The MoF now includes in the yearly budget contingent liabilities and aims to limit quasi-fiscal activities (excluding still-used government-held shares to recapitalize SOEs). However, on the negative side, to deteriorating fiscal transparency should be added difficulties with access to information on tax expenditures, which are generally released on a rather ad hoc basis and thus rarely properly or fully scrutinized.

In the fourth area – i.e. intergovernmental relations – it should be noted that the MoF has implemented a new classification of revenues, expenditures, and foreign sources of financing, compatible with European regulations. Apart from developing an IT system of reporting for local government, this improves transparency standards in the area of intergovernmental relations.

Point (5) in the fiscal transparency questionnaire covers audit functions and the position of the MoF in the budgeting process. In the Polish public sector there exist institutions liable to both external and internal audit. At the central government level external audits are performed by the Supreme Chamber of Control (NIK). NIK inspects the accounts of central government and non-budget funds and it examines financial compliance with budgetary legislation. It should be noted that the institution is politically independent, which increases its credibility and its function. At the local government level external audit functions are performed by both NIK and regional clearing chambers. Inspections are effective, although there are some problems with bureaucratic irregularities. The internal audit at both central and local government levels is provided by a systematically developing service: the internal audit programme was started in 2001 and the authorities have increased the number of certified auditors and consequently control units to cover an increasing number of public sector entities.

The MoF has a dominant position in the central government budgeting process. The majority of public entities estimate their budgets based on expenditures limits, which they pass on to the MoF. Limits are based on total revenue projections and the deficit limits to finance them. The impact of deficits on debt dynamics has been analysed in recent years when the risk of exceeding the constitutional debt limit increased. The impact of the MoF on the budgeting process also depends to a certain extent on public sector centralization. In 2004, a new law on public entities' finance was passed, significantly increasing local government contributions to general government spending. However, local government is bound by fiscal rules that are more restrictive than for the central government.

The case of Poland provides impressive examples of fiscal policy rules. The Polish constitution and Act on Public Finances impose debt and deficit rules. There are also examples of similar boundaries connected with the external (European) obligations imposed on Poland. Some expenditure rules have also been introduced ad hoc by the Minister of Finance (known as the 'Belka rules').

Debt rules are the most rigid and effective type of rules. The first is the constitutional limit on public debt, including warranties and guarantees, stipulating that it cannot exceed 60 per cent of GDP. However, the constitution does not contain a definition of public debt and refers to the Act on Public Finances. This gives plenty of room for interpretation in defining debt and can be seen as its main drawback. The second debt rule (in fact, a group of rules) is included in the Act on Public Finances. This regulation binds the government to stay within three public debt thresholds. These are set to halt increases in borrowing restrictions for central and local governments when the public debt to GDP ratio exceeds them. The first limit is set at a debt: GDP ratio of 50 per cent. Exceeding this level obliges central government to maintain a budget deficit: revenue ratio in the next year at the same level as in the year before. The same applies to local government. If public debt exceeds 55per cent of GDP the government is obliged to prepare the next year's budget to be in balance, which necessarily lowers the government's debt: GDP ratio. The government is also obliged to present to Parliament its fiscal consolidation program aimed at decreasing the public debt: GDP ratio. The thresholds for local government deficits have also been tightened. The last threshold is equal to the constitutional limit for public debt (60per cent of GDP). The third debt limit is also compatible with the Maastricht criteria. If public debt reaches or exceeds such a level, the next year's budget for central and local governments must be balanced. Additionally, warranties and guarantees granted by public sector units are prohibited. The government is also obliged to present to Parliament a fiscal consolidation program aimed at reducing the public debt: GDP ratio.

If debt exceeds the first threshold it has rather limited consequences for fiscal policy. An increase of debt above 55per cent of GDP, which to some extent would force the government to balance the central budget, would have a wider impact on central and local budgets. One of the main disadvantages of debt rules is the two-year delay between the date of breaching the debt limit and the obligation to implement a remedy.

The Polish constitution contains a clause that the central government budget deficit cannot be changed without parliamentary approval. The government therefore tends to prepare a rather cautious forecast of revenues and expenditures in its budget projections. The government has also sometimes been forced to have recourse to creative accounting procedures or to allow excessive lending by non-budget institutions to reach previously envisaged deficit levels. This has usually taken place if the performance of revenues has been worse than assumed and stems largely from the high share of fixed expenditure in the budget.

After its accession to the Union, Poland has had to comply with SGP restrictions on its fiscal deficit. The SGP states that the general government deficit cannot exceed 3per cent of GDP. If this level is breached members are supposed to be subject to excessive deficit procedures. Moreover, the threshold of 3per cent of GDP is also one of the convergence criteria and consequently will be a long-term fiscal goal, given the declarations made by the Polish authorities of their intention to enter EMU as quickly as possible.

Poland has made significant progress in putting fiscal transparency into practice. However, the most challenging areas for achieving IMF and EU standards remain medium-term budgeting as well as accounting and data quality. The most important benefits in terms of transparency of policy in Poland would be an improvement in the fiscal management process, which would be especially beneficial to the convergence path.

One of the most widely recommended changes in fiscal policy should be the implementation of an MTBF, which would provide compatibility between the budgeting process and medium-term fiscal goals (for example, those included in the convergence reports). This would reinforce government attempts to meet fiscal convergence criteria and thus also increase credibility. Budget planning based on medium-term macroeconomic projections would also increase public finance stability if macroeconomic risk was included.

Because of decentralization of government activities – mainly by increasing the share of local budgets in the general government sector – compatible accounting and reporting systems should be established in order to effectively monitor fiscal risk and analyse sustainability. Establishing a new law on local government revenues increases local entities' flexibility and responsibility in the spending policy. Essential knowledge in the sphere of budgeting should be transferred to local governments in order to avoid fiscal problems similar to those the central government experienced, when the first cyclical slowdown took place between 2001 and 2002.

The fiscal rules distinguish Poland positively among central European countries in terms of protection from fiscal expansion. The most rigid are the debt rules, which reduce the risks of excessive borrowing and uncontrolled increases in debt servicing, which would result in constraining public spending or default. Debt rules constitute the ultimate limit for government borrowing, which becomes active when debt reaches a ceiling. Deficit rules should be treated as a current constraint on fiscal policy. On the one hand, overrigid deficit rules in transition countries can cause additional turbulence for policy-making due to high volatility of output. On the other hand, deficit rules, which are valid in Poland, do not guarantee essential and effective motivation for the government to maintain a healthy public finance position. Concerning rules binding local government one should note that they are strictly more rigid than for central government. This could also lead to recourse to creative accounting by local government and this would suggest that internal and external audits, as well as the implementation of comparable accounting and reporting methods, should be carried out.

Notes

1. Based on Hölscher and Stephan (2004). This study was elaborated within the contexts of the two projects: 'Is merger control too lax in transition countries?', ACE-Project P97-8020-R and 'EU integration and the prospects for catch-up

development in CEECs: the determinants of the productivity gap', EU 5th Framework Programme HPSE-CT-2001–00065.
2. In their negotiation positions, accession countries frequently specify that most of the rules in the *acquis* will be directly applicably only from the date of accession.
3. After all, issues raised in chapters are often interlinked and can reappear in other chapters such as state aid for environmental business projects in the chapter on 'competition policy' and the chapter on 'environment'.
4. This share is not statutory.
5. This appears to follow the example of the North American Free Trade Area (NAFTA), where harmonization of competition law was initiated, but enforcement of the law lies still with the national authorities.
6. Based on Benecki, Hölscher and Jarmuzek (2005).
7. Foreign debt was incurred in the 1970s when successive communist governments borrowed to finance unsuccessful manufacturing sector reforms.

References and further reading

Allan, W., Parry, T. (2003) Fiscal Transparency in EU Accession Countries: Progress and Future Challenges, IMF Working Papers, International Monetary Fund.

Benecki, R., J. Hölscher and M. Jarmuzek (2006) Fiscal transparency and policy rules in Poland, in P. Jaworski and T. Mickiewicz (eds), *Polish EU Accession in Comparative Perspective: Macroeconomics, Finance and the Government* (University College London, Occasional Papers London: UCL).

Hölscher, J. and J. Stephan (2004) 'Competition policy in Central East Europe in the light of EU accession', *Journal of Common Market Studies* 42 (2), 321–45.

Stephan, J. (ed.) (2005) *Technology Transfer via Foreign Direct Investment in Central and Eastern Europe – Theory, Method of Research and Empirical Evidence*, (Basingstoke: Palgrave).

9
Country Case Studies

East Germany: the transfer economy

The size of transfers

The treaty on the economic, currency, and social union with the Federal Republic of Germany (West Germany) of 1 July 1990 implanted the West German economic and social constitution almost instantly in the GDR. The *economic union* imposed the constitution that ruled the West German market economy including the common law of the European Union on a socialist CPE. The *social union* introduced the West German set of social entitlements to the GDR – the pension system, the unemployment benefits, the health system. The *currency union* made the D-Mark the legal tender in East Germany and regulated the conversion of the East German Mark. This import of West Germany formal institutions was more or less finished when the GDR acceded to the Federal Republic on 3 October 1990 and was transformed into the 5 new federal states of Germany. East Germany was included in the European Union, the Union's first eastern enlargement.

Compared with all other former socialist countries, East Germany is a special case of transformation, with respect to three aspects:

- The GDR was the only socialist country that started and completed transformation within the same year (1990).
- No other transition country experienced a collapse in its industrial output of an order of approximately 35 per cent within the two years 1990 and 1991 (see Figure 9.1)
- No other country received and still receives financial assistance or transfers from 'abroad' in order to compensate the income losses from transition.

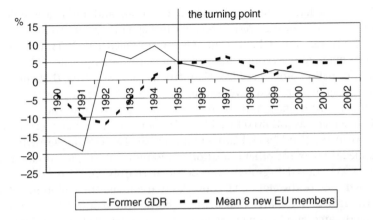

Figure 9.1 East Germany: GDP growth rates in comparison with new EU members,
ᵃ1990–2002

Note:
ᵃ Unweighted means: Czech Republic, Estonia, Hungary, Latvia, Lithuania, Poland, Slovakia, and Slovenia.

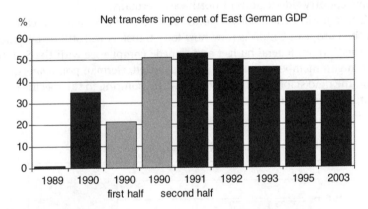

Figure 9.2 Net transfers in relation to East German GDP, 1989–2003 (GDP = 100)
Source: Halle Institute for Economic Research.

Entitlements from the social union rules generated a substantial flow of income transfers to old-age pensioners, the unemployed, or persons in need. Additional transfers resulted from the regulations of the economic union, from privatisation and other, initially unexpected, impacts of unification. Financial support was some 50 per cent of East German

GDP immediately after the economic, social, and monetary union between the GDR and West Germany (the FRG) in July 1990 (Figure 9.2). Transfers were still at 35 per cent of East German GDP in 2003. The assistance made many economists and politicians initially believe that the transformation problem of East Germany was almost solved, that emigration would stop and living standards would catch-up with West Germany. And, indeed, the two year output collapse after the systemic changeover was followed by a blooming of the East Germany economy between 1992 and 1994. During that time, the East German growth rate topped those of the other transition economies. But the picture changed in 1995. The GDP growth rate declined sharply and fell below the growth rate of the eight CEE countries that entered the Union in 2004. GDP growth rates even fell behind the persistent low West German growth rates, and income convergence came to a halt. The East German unemployment rate was higher than that of the 2004 new EU members (Figure 9.3).[1] And despite the impressively high living standards of East German citizens, emigration could not be halted and more and more younger people who see a better perspective outside of East Germany leave; younger people seem to have disappeared almost completely in some country side regions of north-east Germany.

The question that worries politicians in Germany and increasingly in the European Union is now how long transfers will still be a burden to the German federal budget and impede compliance with the SGP by the largest member state of the Union. Indeed, German politicians question the rigid stability criteria of the SGP by pointing to the specific fiscal burden of unification.

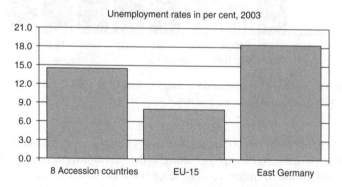

Figure 9.3   East German unemployment rates in comparison, 2003

A copy of the West German pattern, and its costs

The economic union had two important effects for the East German economy. First, it abandoned all import restrictions, and the relative prices of West Germany applied. The value added of most former GDR industries necessarily turned negative: the prices of imported raw material increased to world market levels, and the prices of East German commodities went down compared with West German ones because of the quality discount. A second important component of the economic union was the adoption of the system of tariff negotiations between trade unions and employers' associations. However, there were no well-established employers' associations in East Germany as in West Germany, and delegates of West German trade unions dominated the newly established regional trade unions in East Germany, so the negotiations could not be fair and balanced. Nominal wages started to catch-up with West German wages; the West German trade unions' interest in eliminating cheap labour competition met with East Germany's belief that the social union's task is to ensure equal life conditions in East and West Germany.

The economic union alone would have put a substantial burden even on a fully fledged market economy. But with their own currency, these economies would have been able to buffer at least a part of the wage rate increase by a currency depreciation or by providing credit to the company sector. With the currency union, East Germany lost both these two important fields of macroeconomic policy. The benefit of the introduction of the D-Mark was nonetheless a very short and moderate period of inflation, while in most other transformation countries inflation was initially at three-digit levels.

But the currency union gave birth to another huge long-run burden on the East German economy: the applied currency conversion rate. If the conversion rate had mirrored the productivity gap between East and West Germany in producing tradable goods, then a conversion of 4 East German Marks into 1 D-Mark would have been correct. However, two problems would have emerged: first, the living standard of the population in any country is not only a result of producing tradable goods, but also of *non-tradable* ones (services). A 1:4 conversion rate would have lowered the living standards of the East German population below the level of all-economy productivity, for the productivity gap in producing non-tradable goods is lower. Such a decline in the living standards was possible in the other transformation countries, but not in a united Germany. The second problem was that with a 1:4 conversion rate, social assistance granted according to the new social system would have exceeded wages and pensions, and created a disincentive to work. The conversion rate was finally set at 1:1 for wages and pensions, and 1:1.8 for savings and other assets. This was a clear overvaluation of the East German currency, violating any equilibrium considerations and damaging the competitiveness of the company sector during and after privatization.

Now one may understand the central economic problem of implanting the constitution of a fully fledged market economy into a former CPE: the increase in the real wage prevented a decline in the relative price of labour compared to energy and capital. Restructuring and catching-up in income terms was not possible via cheap labour as in other transformation countries. Having a choice between wage subsidies in order to ease wage cost pressures on enterprises (suggested by Akerlof *et al.* 1991) and subsidies to investment, the federal government voted for the latter. This concept was based on the belief that a catching-up of labour productivity with wages would lead out of the cost dilemma. Assume labour productivity to depend on the capital stock, and income in a fixed relation to the capital stock, then restructuring and modernization of the capital stock was the only option for the East German economy to bring productivity and costs into balance. All the technologies and methods used in West Germany for improving labour productivity should have been made available also to East Germany. The quick privatization of the state-owned enterprises, and transfers to the enterprise sector were the main tools.

The cost of privatization

In July 1990, the privatization agency (the *Treuhandanstalt*) counted 8,000 state-owned enterprises in industry, 30,000 detail and wholesale units, thousands of pharmacies and libraries, and 19 million ha of farmland, forests, and lakes. By splitting up these enterprises the number of units to be privatized in industry, increased from 8,000 to almost 14,000, of which only sixty-five remained to privatization by the end of December 1994. The main privatization method was outsider privatization, that is the direct sale to West German companies and foreign investors. Only 18 per cent of plants were MBOs. About 27 per cent of the initial stock of companies was liquidated because of the poor prospects of these units.

The cost of privatization was the once and forever forgone budget revenues from privatization, which could not be used for public investment into infrastructure. The value of the capital stock was initially estimated at about 310 billion D-Mark. However, privatization was completed with a deficit of about 236 billion D-Mark, increasing public debt – that is, debt shifted to the West German taxpayer. Why did the actual revenues from privatization so grotesquely differ from expected ones? The answer is simple: to obtain the *present* value of a company the *future* value has to be discounted by applying the expected profit rate, for which prices and costs need to be estimated with some certainty. The problem was similar in all transition countries: the uncertainty about the development and stability of institutions was the main obstacle to privatization, and the problem was alleviated by gradual privatization in other countries. Privatization in East Germany was quick and linked to the hope that the imposition of West German institutions would pro-vide sufficient certainty to potential investors. However, in East Germany investors were not able to formulate reliable expectations about the future profitability of state-owned companies under the spe-cific circumstances of East German transformation – above all the effects of currency union and the present value of companies in the light of the West German legal environment (for example, environmental regula-tions). Therefore, the privatization agency could not apply methods such as vouchers or auctions. The privatization agency decided on nego-tiations with prospective investors, evaluating not only the offered price but also investment plans and employment commitments.

The negative revenue from privatization was tantamount to an implicit asset transfer that the government channelled to investors. To this add massive payments in preparing state-owned companies for privatization – for example in the elimination of environmental damage. Nothing remained for investment in public infrastructure from the GDR's family silver. The modernization and construction of an infra-structure in traffic and telecommunications had to be financed by transfers from federal and other West German public budgets to East German public entities. Finally, many enterprises – privatized as well as newly established – needed public support to survive the first years in a macroeconomic environment which was hostile in terms of high relative capital costs. In 2003, about 11 per cent of all transfer payments were still direct subsidies to the enterprise sector.

The social and economic effects of transfers

Transfers certainly fulfil social functions: while GDP per capita was at about 64 per cent of the West German level in 2003, transfers raised the disposable income of households to about 86 per cent. Although (relative) poverty was at a somewhat higher level in East Germany than in West Germany, social transfers prevented mass poverty. The actual winners from German unification were old-age pensioners: net old age pensions achieved the West German level in 1995.[2] However, the economic effects were dubious.

The problem of transfers is very close to the problem of foreign aid, which is one of the major topics in the development literature. There is a broad library dealing with the question what undermines aid's impact on growth (recently: Rajan and Subramanian, 2005). While one strand of this literature focuses on the effects of aid/transfers on the real exchange rate of the receiving country, another, more institutional strand discusses how efficiency is affected. The former couples with the *Dutch Disease* phenomenon, the latter with the phenomenon of the soft budget constraint. The term 'Dutch Disease' originated in Holland after the discovery of North Sea gas in the 1960s. It means the slump in manufacturing industries that occurs when the discovery of a natural resource raises the value of a nation's currency, making manufactured goods less competitive, increasing imports, and decreasing exports. The East Germany's 'natural resource' was its 'rich brother', the FRG. Even the expectation of revenue – as in East Germany before unification – might trigger a Dutch Disease syndrome.

Another effect is the macroeconomic *'soft' budget constraint* on the East German economy. In the development literature, the results of aid to a poor country are known as the 'crowding out' of domestic savings by foreign savings. Domestic economic agents do not find the incentive to increase revenues and savings from their own activity. In the East German context, the effect was somewhat different: not managers of companies, but regional authorities expected to obtain further finance from the federal budget and from other public budgets, when their revenues from formerly supported private investment projects fell short of the expected tax revenues. There was a lack of competition between states and between local authorities in obtaining financial assistance from the federal budget, and for a substantial part of East German business investment was financed by transfers via public households; the market mechanism in the private company sector was thus severely hampered in its selection function. East Germany was transformed from a centrally planned to a transfer economy.

Hungary: the economy of stop–go cycles

Contrast of hope and reality

The suppression of the Hungarian Revolution against the soviet influence in 1956 was followed by a period of severe repression proving also that a major change either in the economic or in the political system was not an option. However, after a decade it seemed that minor reforms could be tolerated. In Hungary an economic reform called the New

Economic Mechanism was implemented in 1968. It was thought to have far-reaching consequences, bringing about a transformation of the economic system unnoticed by the soviets. This was however not the case. The centrally planned system remained in place, while elements of a market economy have been introduced. Against early hopes, this could not lead far without changing the main structure, the institutions and the incentives. Being a mixture of things, this was widely named the 'Goulash Communism'.[3] It did lead to a true market economy (a first blasted hope), but was definitely the most open system in the region, where economic agents had an experience with some market mechanisms much earlier than the system was changed.

According to this 'advantage' many hoped that the regime change would not have such severe consequences as elsewhere, and that transition can be smoother since the economy will be able to adapt faster. This could again not come true. First, the transformational recession could not be avoided as most of the economy has been built on an artificial basis (not taking into account the country's comparative advantages), market had to be introduced and the system completely changed so that decision makers have the right incentives, which was not the case under the Hungarian 'third way', and not least the country had to face a serious problem of managing its high levels of debt. In the 1970s Hungary started to borrow heavily in order to pay for its risen import costs due to the oil price increases. In fear of losing access to foreign funds the country wanted to build up a reputation of being a good debtor, so insisted on honouring its debt instead of asking for reduction or rescheduling as Poland, Bulgaria or Russia did for example. This however put strong constrains on the Hungarian opportunities of development. Obviously the restructuring required enormous amounts of financial aid, but due to the high debt levels the government lacked the means, while capital markets were still reluctant to lend because of the perceived high credit risk.

Hope and disappointment was thus a cycle the society went through repeatedly – in parallel with the stop–go cycles of the economy. This is true for the whole period, resulting in a deep loss of credibility, with politicians creating undue hopes again and again and a growing disappointment over time. A loss of patience definitely dose not help a process of transformation. Whenever the authorities thought that the worst might be over and time had come to reap the benefits, they had to face the harsh reality, only exacerbating the original problem by this approach. Thinking that they know better, that there was a third, a Hungarian, a different, and a better way did not help, when all the evidence seemed to suggest the opposite.

Microeconomic restructuring and bad macroeconomic performance

When Hungary entered the Union in May 2004, it had a private sector share of GDP (80 per cent) and employment (85 per cent), among the highest of the transformation countries. The social system had been reformed in the 1990s, including the introduction of private pension funds. Nevertheless, Hungary's economy had never experienced the expected high growth rates of GDP or GDP *per capita* over a sustained period. This discrepancy between fast transformation and reform and the results was partly due to exogenous factors, but mostly to macroeconomic mistakes (often having political causes), creating unnecessary cycles in the development process.

After the change in political system, a rapid economic restructuring had to start to lay the ground for a stable growth path. Having contracted by 3.5 per cent in 1990, GDP shrank by 12 per cent in 1991 and another 3 per cent in 1992. Growth reappeared only in 1994 (3 per cent), after a further small reduction of GDP by 0.6 per cent in 1993 (see Figure 9.4). There was only a slow decrease in inflation while the inherited high level of government debt increased to 80 per cent by 1992.

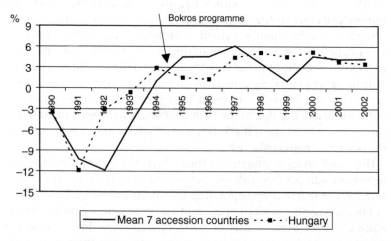

Figure 9.4 Hungary: GDP growth rates in comparison with other new EU members,[a] 1990–2002

Note:
[a] Unweighted means: Czech Republic, Estonia, Hungary, Latvia, Lithuania, Poland, Slovakia, and Slovenia.

While the government advocated a gradual approach, rapid change took place at the microeconomic level supported by the reshaping of many institutions and new market legislation. Several elements had in fact been initiated before the regime change. The two-tier banking system stems from 1987 and the Act on Companies and Business Undertakings from 1988. In 1990 a Law on Securities was passed regulating the stock exchange. In 1991 the Act on Credit Institutions and another on the National Bank of Hungary were passed, the latter limiting the possibilities for monetization of public debt. The most important of all was the Bankruptcy Law and the accompanying Act On accounting, erecting very tough requirements on companies, effectively hardening their budget constraint virtually over night.[4] Other countries opted for a slower selection of viable firms while temporarily tolerating the existence of unviable firms. In just a few months most Hungarian companies had been restructured, which improved the financial situation, but a tenth of them went bust with all the dire consequences for economic activity, output, and unemployment.

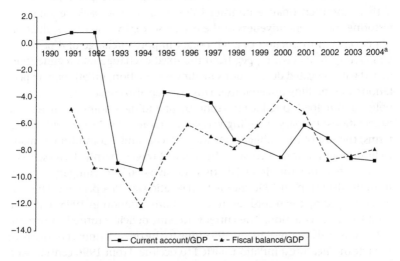

Figure 9.5   Hungary: current account and budget balance, 1990–2004, per cent of GDP

Note:
[a] 2004 figure is a preliminary estimate, still subject to amendment. The fiscal balance is recalculated including the debt of SOEs. According to the previously followed methodology, the current account balance slightly exceeded the fiscal balance in 1993–1994.

Source: National Bank of Hungary (throughout this study).

Contrary to initial expectations, the growth of the Hungarian economy did not outpace the average of the other new member states in transition: it was either well below, or very close to, their average level. However, with an improving current account the government thought that the time had come to stimulate the economy and set growth as a top priority. Macroeconomic policy became expansive in 1993–1994 (the latter also being an election year). Increased spending further worsened the budgetary situation, driving the debt: GDP ratio to 90 per cent by 1993. Lax monetary policy resulted in low interest rates and the decrease of household savings, so that the current account turned into massive deficit. (This twin deficit can be seen in Figure 9.5) Inflation started to rise again in 1994 (also due to an increase in value added tax, VAT, and excise taxes, which was aimed at creating higher budget revenues to limit the deficit). By the end of the year, the situation was no longer sustainable and radical policy measures were needed to avoid serious financial problems.

Stabilization package, March 1995: avoiding a second crisis

After some hesitation the government accepted a package of austerity measures widely known as the Bokros package (after the name of its 'father', the then finance minister Lajos Bokros). The package aimed at restoring the competitiveness of the export sector by a sharp devaluation (9 per cent), introduction of a temporary import surcharge of 8 per cent, and change to a crawling peg from the fixed exchange rate regime (burdened with repeated devaluations fuelling speculation, inflationary expectations, and fuelling uncertainty). This last step also constrained monetary policy and helped to reduce inflation by providing a nominal anchor for expectations. Primary spending was cut by more than 15 per cent in real terms, the size of the public sector was reduced, and a commitment made to limit nominal wage increases. In fact, real wages sharply decreased as a consequence, but the financial crisis was avoided and Hungary escaped from the debt trap: in 1996 the debt: GDP ratio was 75.4 per cent. This was much helped by the record revenues from privatization in 1995 that were used for debt reduction. The current account deficit returned to sustainable levels and after peaking in 1995 (due to the one-off impact of many of the reform measures) inflation started to decline. From 1996 central bank financing of government deficits was completely ruled out. But the economy responded relatively fast (attributed to the great extent of restructuring accomplished at the beginning of the 1990s) and in 1997 the best period in Hungary's growth history began: for four consecutive years the growth rate exceeded 4 per cent (staying close to 5 per cent in two of them). Compared with other seven accession countries, Hungary adjusted its economy earlier in order to avoid a financial crisis, and therefore the slowing down of output was less pronounced compared with the general downswing in the second half of the 1990s in the other countries. Adjustment costs were far higher, for example, in the Czech Republic after the financial crisis of 1997, when GDP declined.

Believing in miracles

Economic developments are very sensitive to external tendencies in Hungary because of the great openness of the country. The global slowdown in the late 1900s, especially in Europe and Germany (the European Union in general and Germany in particular are the main trading partners of Hungary) clouded economic prospects. The government wanted to keep the growth rate high, so tried to switch to domestic demand as the main driving force of the economy and consequently loosened its fiscal policy stance significantly. To ease social tensions, nominal wages were also increased sharply, especially in the public sector, resulting in a 12–13 per cent increase in real wages in 2002, while labour productivity increase was a modest 4.5 per cent. This coupled a strong fiscal deficit with a current account deficit of the same order of magnitude once again (Figure 9.6).

At the same time, monetary policy became increasingly restrictive. After the decrease of inflation slowed (partly due to external factors), the bands

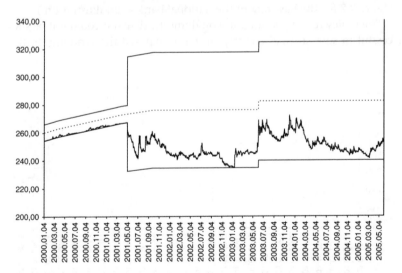

Figure 9.6 The Forint in the Hungarian exchange rate system (HUF/EUR, from 2000)

of the exchange rate system widened to ±15 per cent (from ±2.25 per cent) in May 2001, and in October the crawling system was abandoned. The more flexible system allowed the National Bank of Hungary to follow a different monetary strategy, and in the summer inflation targeting was introduced. Aiming at keeping to its announced targets and counteracting the inflationary effects of fiscal policy, the central bank kept interest rates relatively high. The exchange rate appreciated strongly (see Figure 9.6 for movements of the nominal exchange rate), for high interest rates attracted debt-creating capital inflows while the share of FDI lost its former dominance in financing the current account deficit.

The result was a speculation on the strong side of the band in January 2003, when the central bank defended the system, but the speculative attack was largely attributable to a loss of credibility partly caused by the inconsistency of fiscal and monetary policy and the outright disputes between the government and the national bank over the correct course of economic policy. The worst was yet to come: under government pressure there was a devaluation (going against the previous reasoning of the president of the central bank) and with the reoccurrence of the twin deficits this resulted in a credibility crisis with a strongly devaluating currency. The central bank stepped in, tightening the monetary conditions once again. This made not only the exchange rate, but also the market interest rates very volatile resulting in growing uncertainty. (see Figure 9.7 for the base rate of the national bank as an illustration.)

The policy relying dominantly on domestic demand could not be successful in such a small country, and also exposed the economy to the

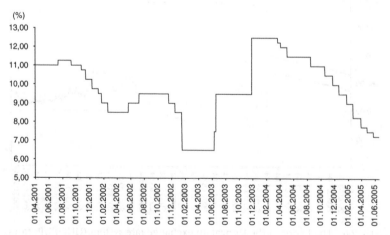

Figure 9.7   Hungary: base rate of the National Bank, 2001–2005

well-known imbalances encountered in the past. The growth rate declined, inflation picked up again and not least the public debt: GDP ratio increased. Having reached 53.5 per cent in 2001 it was up to 57.9 per cent in 2002 and 59.1 per cent in 2003. Correction was needed once more.

If the current environment of a political fight for power as whatever means is not rapidly replaced by quick action and careful policy aiming at sustainable development, Hungary will not be able to make use of the opportunities related to EU accession: the price already paid for the transformation of the economy will definitely prove to be too high. There is no easy way: change in politics on both sides is urgently needed in the direction of increased realism and credibility.

Russia: the oligarchic economy

The rise of the oligarchs

Russia is the most important successor state of the Soviet Union, for it inherited the USSR's economic and military potential, as well as its foreign debt of about $120 billion in 1992 and a huge debt service exceeding the foreign exchange reserves of the country. The Gajdar programme of 1992 followed the 'shock-like' transition concept adopted in Poland and other countries. It included the liberalization of prices, of trade and banking, establishment of a central bank, privatization, and consolidation of state finance (stabilization). Most of the small-scale enterprises, and 80 per cent of the large-scale enterprises in the manufacturing sector were privatized on a legal base by means of a privatization law predominantly by vouchers by the end of 1994. There were some important exceptions from liberalization and privatization: the energy and raw material sectors were initially not included in privatization and price liberalization, and this created the basis for the rise of the oligarchs. Economic growth resumed only in 1999, after a severe financial crisis (Figure 9.8). Until then, Russia was plagued by the threat of hyperinflation, disintegration, and the breakdown of public finances. The oligarchs benefited from this development and they contributed to one of the most dangerous situations of a transition country–capital flight.

The roots of the oligarchs can actually be found in the late Soviet Union period. When Michael Gorbachev took power in 1985, the economy was already approaching breakdown. The Soviet system had lost its ability to 'mobilise revenue for the state at the expense of the consumption standards of the ordinary population' (Olson 1993). A class of state enterprise directors, of bureaucrats and party leaders, the so-called *nomenklatura*, depleted the rich natural resources of the Soviet

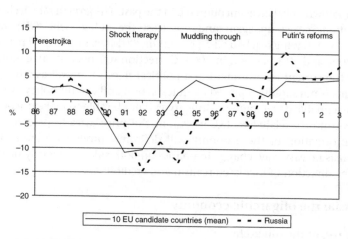

Figure 9.8   Real GDP development, per cent, as against previous year: Russia and EU candidate countries, 1986–2003

Union, which had former been 'people's property' but were actually at the disposal of the *nomenklatura*. With the Gorbachev reforms, rent-seeking was no longer an illegal business. *Perestroika* implanted more autonomy and self-government in regions and SOEs; decentralization should have made the economy more efficient. However, this intention failed since it abolished central control only, but not central planning and the prevalence of state ownership. The opportunities for rent-seeking and SBC widened significantly. Many managers of SOEs, and many bureaucrats in the state administration or communist mass organizations, took their first steps in the accumulation of huge wealth, very often protected by high-level party leaders and their clans. With still state administered prices, the directors could sell the output of their enterprise to 'front firms' and 'straw men' at the low domestic price, and then resell it at world prices (the foreign trade controls were already relaxed). This practice was continued even after the 1992 price liberalization, for state price controls remained in the oil, gas, and metal sectors. A new class of super-rich individuals emerged, who founded *pocket banks* to hold the money. The banks provided financing to the state budget; here were the roots for the increasing dependence of political parties and government members. Spontaneous privatization or 'asset-stripping' was common, and the accumulated money wealth was stored in pocket banks while a beneficial financial investment was found. When in 1995 the Yeltsin government was cash-strapped (low tax collection, the war in Chechnya, and heavy subsidies to failing industries), and elections were in 1996, banks proposed to upcoming loan funds with repayment secured by the government's majority stake in the key strategic industries that had been excluded from voucher privatization. The government auctioned control over its shares in lucrative metals, oil, and other sectors (the automotive industry, for example) in return for the loans, giving the shares as security to whomever lent it the most money.

The process was inefficient and non-transparent in a number of ways:

- First, foreigners were barred from participating, showing that this was to be, as – a former Russian minister put it, a case of 'the oligarchs splitting up companies among old friends.'
- Second, the right to manage the auctions was parcelled out among the major banks, which managed to win the auctions they were appointed to manage with bids at or just above the minimum price.
- Third, the bidding was rigged by having affiliates of the bank organizing the auction submit 'rival' bids and excluding bids on 'technical grounds'. Loans-for-shares had the important corollary that it was not just a give-away of state property; it was a trade of state property for political support.

President Yeltsin failed to find an orderly way to a civic society in Russia after the fall of the Soviet Union. The Soviet dictatorship was simply replaced by the collapse of order; the threat of nationalization of private property by the communist state was replaced by the threat of private robbery (either through spontaneous 'privatization' or direct violence). The signs of increasing disorder included the transformation of the criminals of the Soviet Union into the 'mafia', the birth of the 'oligarchs', and the successful struggle the of the regions (republics, etc.) for more independence from Moscow. Since the Gajdar reforms had excluded oil and other resources from price liberalization, the opportunities for rent-seeking widened even more under the new liberal environment. Yeltsin's aim to win many battles with the Russian communists had a high price: in the 1993 constitution, the eighty-nine members of the Russian federation received financial autonomy which had the consequence of increasing local budget deficits from 1994 to 1997. In 1996, new banks provided financial assistance to Yeltsin's struggle against communists in exchange for shares in strategic industries, which were not yet privatized. The oligarchs demonstrated their power and dominance in Russian policies.

The 'new rich' and capital flight

However, the prospects of defending the new wealth were initially very uncertain, and the class of 'new rich' tried to transfer a part of its wealth abroad. The size of capital flight from Russia is estimated to have been enormous, especially in the years prior to 1999 (between $14 and $36 billion in 1996 and 1997 (Tikhomirov 1997). These estimates stood for about 11–27 per cent of Russia's gross foreign debt.

It is a tricky task to disentangle capital flight from normal capital export. Normal capital export includes debt repayment, direct investment abroad, or loans financing exports. A normal capital export can also occur with portfolio investment. When investors wish to rebalance their portfolio owing to factors such as a financial crisis in another region of the world, the outflow of capital can hardly be called capital flight. Compared with most CEE transition countries, where the current and capital accounts have been already liberalized, Russia maintained many controls on foreign exchange movements. With a restricted capital account, capital flight occurred with fake invoicing of exports of raw material and energy. Fake invoicing means that – with free trade – domestic firms establish a middleman firm abroad, and sell to it at submarket prices. The middleman firm re-sells at the world market price. The rent is held in a foreign bank. In November 2000, the Russian Federal Ministry of Finance and the Federal Tax Police issued a report showing that oil companies had sold to affiliate offshore trading companies at submarket prices. The report said that the state was losing $9 billion a year (about 5 per cent of GDP) in tax receipts. This example demonstrated how the political power of big oil companies prevented the tax authorities from punishing such practices.

Stabilization policy in a disintegrating economy

One of the uncertainties that led to capital flight was the threat of *hyperinflation*. The strong inflationary pressure could initially not be handled by a restrictive monetary policy based on a nominal exchange rate anchor as in the other transformation countries. The other successor states of the Soviet Union created their own currency and the rouble started to flow back into Russia, jeopardizing the remaining foreign exchange reserves of the central bank. With free prices for most manufactured and consumer goods, and a devaluing rouble, Russia was on the way to hyperinflation. Since 1994 a new threat also emerged: the ruin of public finances. The reformers were ambivalent insofar as they hesitated to accept mass insolvency of the state-owned sector and mass unemployment threatened – the consequences of the 'shock approach' plus the breakdown of foreign trade. The deficit in the consolidated state budget increased in 1992 and 1993 through tax evasion and poor tax collection, the latter often a result of generous tax exemption for large oil companies. In particular, the deficits in the budgets of the members of the Russian federation increased. The central government was not able to impose effective control on the central and local budgets; short-term T-bills and medium-term bonds financed their deficits. The commercial banks were allowed to borrow abroad and to finance the purchase of bills and bonds. The federal government desperately tried to consolidate public finances by not paying a part of the wages and pensions in the public sector. A severe commitment problem spread across the Russian economy: everybody tried to avoid tax payments or to pay bills, and barter mushroomed. Foreign support, provided mainly by IMF credits, merely sufficed to cover the capital flight.

In 1998, with a low world market price for oil, the traditional current account surplus dwindled and the lenders' confidence into Russian debtors – in particular, the federal government – shrank. With an increasing interest rate, the market price of bills and bonds dropped; the crisis spread from the fiscal to the banking sector. In the second half of August 1998, the pegged rouble collapsed. Russia interrupted the repayment of some external debt, the state bank pumped money into the banking system, and inflation soared. Inflation moderated again in 1999, and GDP recovered for the first time since 1991. World oil and metal prices started to increase and eased the external and domestic financial situation. The crisis paved the way for a consolidation of federal debt and of the banking sector, but it was clear that something had to be done in order to halt the process of social, political, and economic disintegration.

The Putin reforms: towards a new social contract or an authoritarian state?

In 2000, a joint statement of Russian (Leonid Abalkin and Nikolai Petrakov) and US economists (among them the noble prize winners Lawrence R. Klein, Franco Modigliani and Douglass North) was addressed to President Putin, stating that a new reform attempt would be necessary to solve two basic problems that the Gajdar programme had neglected: *legal uncertainty*, and the *moral crisis* of the society. Indeed, it was a profound misconception that a 'shock-like' approach could fit Russia with its imperial history, its regional, national, and cultural diversities, and without an effective social safety net. Gajdar's concept not only accounted for the 'normal' transition shock, it created

---

Box 9.1   The YUKOS affair

In 2003, Mikhail Khodorkovsky, the CEO of the YUKOS company was taken in custody. The Putin government claimed that YUKOS did not pay taxes – a widespread behaviour of large Russian enterprises in the Yeltsin era, tolerated by the government. YUKOS denied this charge. Many political commentators understood the move against the company as an attempt by Putin to suppress political opposition by the threat of renationalization. Headquartered in Moscow, YUKOS is one of Russia's largest publicly traded oil and gas companies, with about 100,000 employees. It was founded in April 1993 out of two former Soviet energy enterprises by a decree of the Russian government. It became the first fully privatized oil company in 1995–1996, in the course of the loan for-shares privatization programme, with the objective of providing the Yeltsin administration with finance for their re-election campaigns. The bank that received the major share package was MENATEP, a 'pocket bank' headed by Mikhail Khodorkovsky. Khodorkovsky, an officer of the then communist youth association KOMSOMOL, was the co-founder of the bank in 1988, when Gorbachev allowed the KOMSOMOL to undertake early 'capitalist' experiments. Successful in restructuring the petroleum industry from ruins to profitability, Khordorkorsky is said to have become the richest person in Russia. His political ambitions qualify him as an 'oligarch', however, related to Putin's political opponents. The manner of the YUKOS company split and renationalization may become a major obstacle for economic reform and the engagement of foreign investors.

---

opportunities for rent-seeking and the depletion of public and private property; it destroyed the government's ability to protect the poor; and it failed to offer a new social contract between government and population, the popular support to underpin far-reaching systemic changes.

Putin's reform programme of June 2000 addressed important aspect such as a new social contract and the restoring of legal certainty. consisted of three important components:

- First, it continued former reforms in some important fields (taxe privatization, business law).
- Second, it included a social dimension (reform of the social insuranc system, promoting education and culture).
- Third, it aimed at the restoration of the federal state in the econom and society (recentralization, reduction of the power of the region structural policy).

The major objective of the new social contract between the state and th society was demonstrated by the prominent position of social reforms.

The major objective of legal certainty was to create incentives for investment into fixed capital. Legal certainty included not only the effectiveness of the business and tax law, but also the fight against crime, and the containment of, corruption and the political power of oligarchs. In particular, the YUKOS affair of 2003–2005 seemed to be an attempt to correct the effects of the spontaneous privatization and rent-seeking of the early years (see Box 9.2). However, in a country with a weak and brief democratic experience, the fight against the oligarchs may turn into the liquidation of the rule of law.

China: currency undervaluation and economic development[5]

Introduction

China was a latecomer to transition, and has pursued a different develop-ment strategy. Here we can treat only one aspect of this strategy: Chinese exchange rate policy, which has become the focus of much debate. The American Secretary of the Treasury, John Snow, in concert with former Federal Reserve Chairmen Alan Greenspan, as well as several Ministers of Finance from Europe, urged the Chinese authorities to implement a more flexible exchange rate system. The Japanese Finance Minister Shiokawa accused China of exporting deflation to the whole Asian region, if not to the world economy, and encouraged the Chinese government to let its currency appreciate. It is not by accident that the discussion of the proper exchange rate system and management, not only of the Chinese ren-minbi but also of most other Asian currencies, evolved at a time of low or moderate growth and rising imbalances in the world economy. The US economy has been experiencing an increasing current account deficit which has reached nearly 5 per cent of GDP and has been mainly driven by the BTC the bilateral trade deficit of the United States with China amounted to $103 billon in 2002 and increased to $120 billion in 2003.

The question of sustainability of the current account deficit seems to be less precarious in the US case. About 90 per cent of US foreign debt is denominated in domestic currency, which offers one additional possibility of eliminating part of the real value of debt by surprise inflation. Of course, 'inflating away' foreign debt is not without its costs. By using this option, the United States would most likely threaten the leading role of the dollar in the world financial system. A more attractive option would be an orderly devaluation of the dollar. Recently, foreign exchange markets seem to have moved in the right direction, the dollar began to depreciate against the Euro, eliminating the overvaluation.

In contrast, market forces for most Asian currencies were weakened by the huge interventions of the Asian central banks. This gave the major part of the work of correcting for global imbalances to the already slow-growing European economies. Against this background, it is of no surprise – that the question of burden-sharing was one major topic of the IMF meeting in Dubai in the autumn of 2003.

Some authors doubt that a revaluation of Asian currencies would be in the best interests of the United States. Japan and China are the biggest foreign investors in US Treasury bonds. If central banks in both countries abstain from further accumulating US bonds, interest rates may rise, thereby depressing economic growth and employment. Although, in principle, this argument seems to be correct, the quantitative dimension should not be exaggerated. China and Japan together hold no more than 10 per cent of all outstanding US government bonds. Therefore, only in the improbable case of a huge sell-off of foreign exchange reserves by the Bank of Japan (BoJ) and the People's Bank of China (PBoC) could the US bond market get into trouble. A moderate shift of the BoJ's and the PBoC's reserves, probably in favour of Euro holdings, as seems to have happened recently, appears to be innocuous considering the huge liquidity of the US market.

Chinese officials, such as the Prime Minister, Wen Jiabao, and the Central Bank Governor, Zhou Xiaochuan, have resisted demands for appreciating the renminbi. Although favouring a more flexible system in principle, they insist that the time is not yet ripe. Moreover, they call into question China's responsibility for the current situation, arguing that western economies, with their unsolved structural problems, are mainly responsible for the imbalances in the world economy.

Reasons for fixing the exchange rate to the US dollar

Many emerging countries have fixed their exchange rate to some international currency or some 'basket' of major currencies. Moreover, many countries which officially let their currency float in fact follow a strategy of 'dirty floating' – i.e. of trying to smooth out fluctuations or establishing some implicit target level or target band for their exchange rate. Notwithstanding the reduction in transaction costs, a major advantage of a fixed exchange rate is the discipline it imposes on monetary policy by reducing the risk of surprise inflation. The first aspect is most important if a government or central bank is trying to establish confidence and reputation in its attempt to disinflate a highly inflationary economy. In this respect, the strict management of the exchange rate since the beginning of 1994 has worked well in the case of China. Consumer price inflation decreased from 25 per cent in 1994 to less then 5 per cent in 1997 and fell further during the Asian crisis to effectively zero. The loss of output remained moderate due to the growth stimulus from net exports following the massive nominal and real devaluation of the renminbi. As the impact of the devaluation on net exports faded out, growth rates of GDP decreased slightly and have since then varied in a range between 5 and 10 per cent per annum.

In the aftermath of the Asian crisis, deflation instead of inflation was the major problem for the monetary policy of the PBoC. But the task of fixing the exchange rate to the dollar was still of importance. The remarkable growth of international trade with double-digit rates – putting aside the Asian crisis – and the huge inflow of FDI was certainly supported by the crisis-proven stability of a still undervalued renminbi exchange rate. Without its unequivocal promise of holding the exchange rate of the renminbi fixed, international investors would probably have been more reluctant in their investment policy. By withstanding any attempt to devalue the renminbi, China made a major contribution to avoiding a process of reciprocal devaluation in Asia during the currency crisis. This was an important prerequisite for the stability of the whole region.

Does the PBoC waste money?

It is quite often argued that the PBoC, by intervening in the forex market, is wasting money. Instead of accumulating low-yielding US Treasury bonds this money could have been used for highly profitable investment projects. This argument seems to be invalid: by intervening in the forex markets the PBoC is buying net foreign assets from commercial banks. Although it is true that a central bank has to follow very cautious investment policy for the use of its reserves, it does not amount to a waste of money because every extra unit of money invested in higher-yielding assets has to be paid by increasing risk. A central bank is not using the full gains of efficiency by diversifying its portfolio if it does not take into account all categories of assets and such losses seem to be too small to be decisive. On the contrary, if the PBoC decided to reduce its holding of reserves and thereby induced a depreciation of the dollar against the renminbi, this would diminish the national currency value of its reserves. Consequently, central bank profit would decline by much more than any realistic estimate of forgone profit. Moreover, and probably most relevant, the decision to appreciate the renminbi has always to take into account the loss of competitiveness and reduced economic growth. Therefore, as long as the Chinese government follows a strategy of export-led growth these macroeconomic considerations will dominate any microeconomic calculation of efficiency loss.

Adjustment of the balance of payments

Irrespective of the undisputed virtues of the fixed parity to the dollar in the past, against the background of mounting problems of controlling monetary and credit growth an adjustment of the renminbi exchange rate to the dollar seems to be the most obvious solution. In principle, there are four different ways that an unavoidable adjustment of the renminbi: dollar exchange rate could materialize:

- Adjustment of the real exchange rate by sticking to the present peg and monetizing the domestic economy (automatic stabilization)
- Discrete revaluation of the exchange rate
- Transition to a regime of floating exchange rates
- Lifting capital controls and facilitating capital exports from the private sector.

The fourth option could, in principle, be combined with a fixed or a floating exchange rate, although experience has shown that in a world of freely moving capital a currency peg is highly vulnerable to speculative attacks. In general, the fourth option should be seen as a complement to rather than a substitute for to the other proposals. We shall therefore discuss this point in the context of the other reform measures.

The first option, obviously, cannot be very attractive to the Chinese government. Having eliminated the former double-digit rates of inflation, the Chinese authorities will not undermine public confidence in the stability of the currency value, since only a quite substantial increase in the inflation rate would bring about the necessary real appreciation. In this case, the negative consequences – in the form of destroyed reputation and a further undermining of the still low confidence in the financial sector, reflected in higher risk premia on interest rates – would clearly outweigh any potential gain. Therefore, the first alternative should clearly be dismissed.

Proponents of the second option – i.e. a discrete revaluation of the renminbi – base their argument on four main propositions:

(1) Under conditions of sufficiently elastic demand (i.e. validity of the Marshall–Lerner condition – or, more generally, the Robinson

condition) an appreciation would reduce the surplus in the current account by making Chinese exports more expensive.

(2) A revaluation would reduce price pressure on competitors in other Asian countries so long as they do not follow suit and hold their currencies in a stable relation to the dollar.

(3) Moreover, a revaluation would make imports cheaper and thereby increase the purchasing power of Chinese consumers, raising their standard of living.

(4) Appreciating the renminbi could at least partially divert FDI from China to other Asian countries. This would be a useful contribution to overcoming the long-lasting effects of the Asian crisis.

At some point in time the Chinese government will have to select a new currency system. Given the vulnerability of the weak financial system, the implementation of a freely floating exchange rate is not a realistic option. Flexible exchange rate arrangements also require an adequate financial infrastructure, with broad and liquid futures markets. As long as these preconditions are not fulfilled, the time is not ripe for the introduction of a floating exchange rate. Therefore, the government has the choice between a one-time – i.e. discretionary – revaluation, a widening of the intervention margin around an unchanged or modified central rate, pegging the renminbi to a broader basket of currencies, or any combination of these.

By sticking to a fixed but appreciated exchange rate, the Chinese authorities could preserve the *anchor function* for investment, trade, and financial markets, including the banking system. In particular, by containing the volatility of the exchange rate, the risk premium in interest rates could be reduced. The major disadvantage of a fixed rate is the lack of flexibility in the case of major shocks. After WTO entry and the expiration of transitional regulations for some sectors of the Chinese economy, competition from foreign companies entering the domestic market should considerably increase. Normally, a smooth and flexible adjustment of market forces to new conditions would be preferable to a discretionary devaluation which – as experience has in many cases proven – is normally too little and too late. Nevertheless, it has to be borne in mind that many real shocks could be corrected by relative price movements and not by a change in the aggregate price level. Therefore, only in the presumably rare cases of major aggregate shocks hitting the economy would an adjustment of the exchange rate be an adequate response. But even in this case, foreign exchange markets characterized by short-termism, irrational behaviour, and other problems do not always pass the test of efficiency.

The higher degree of flexibility may call for a solution with fixed parities surrounded by a symmetric fluctuation margin. In principle, this solution should combine the advantages of fixed rates without sacrificing too much flexibility. Unfortunately, experience with this kind of solution is far from convincing. The stabilization function of upper and lower boundaries of the exchange rate band depend on the credibility of the arrangement. The dilemma then is that whereas the credibility of the target zone increases with the width of the band, the anchor function for expectations declines. Because the role of the exchange rate in stabilizing expectations seems to be more important as long as restrictions on international movements of capital continue to exist, the costs of widening the fluctuation margin seem to outweigh their use.

From a theoretical perspective, the answer largely depends on the concept of economic development. As long as China follows a strategy of export-led growth combined with a surplus on current account a 10 per cent appreciation of the renminbi seems to be the upper bound. This follows from the general rule of thumb that in case of considerable uncertainty about data, the appropriate model, and the implications of policy action, a solution which avoids disaster should be chosen. Depending on circumstances, a more gradual or a very aggressive policy could be appropriate. In case of the Chinese exchange rate policy, the economic and social costs of an overvalued renminbi seem to outweigh an increase in the inflation rate. Correspondingly, a more cautious policy with a moderate revaluation of the renminbi should be preferred to a 'big leap'. China should take the opportunity to adopt a policy which secures internal price stability without endangering job creation and economic growth.

Notes

1. In view of the many instruments reducing registered unemployment in Germany, a so-called 'underemployment' is calculated, 22 per cent in 2003 compared with 18 per cent unemployment. The instruments are: the 'second labour market' (state employment programmes); re-training programmes; early old-age pensions, and other market instruments.
2. The relation of old-age pensions to wage incomes in total household incomes increased from 22 per cent to 34 per cent between 1993 and 1998. This relation remained fairly stable at 19 per cent in West Germany. Data are calculated using *Statistisches Bundesamt*, Fachserie 15, Heft 6: Einkommensverteilung in Deutschland.
3. 'The Hungarian goulash of macroeconomic control was a mixture of political command, licensing, ethical and political suasion, and the application of

economic parameters in both transparent and non-transparent ways.' *Gács* (2000), p. 2.
4. Most of these laws were subsequently modified or replaced in 1996 and again in 2001.
5. Based on Sommer (2005).

References and further reading

Akerlof, G., A.K. Rose, J.L. Yellen and H. Hassenius (1991) 'East Germany in from the cold: the economic aftermath of currency union', *Brookings Papers on Economic Activity* 1, 1–105.

Aslund, Anders (1999) *Why has Russias Transformation been so Ardous?* Paper prepared for the annual World Bank conference on Development Economics, (Washington, DC: World Bank).

Calvo, G. and C. M. Reinhart (2000) 'Fear of floating', *Quarterly Journal of Economics.* 117(2), 379–408.

De Grauwe, (1996), *International Money – Postwar Trends and Theories*, 2nd edn (Oxford: Oxford University Press).

Deutsche Bundesbank (1994), *Monthly Report*, May.

Djankov, S., E. Glaeser, R. La Porta, F. Lopez-de-Silanes and A. Shleifer (2003) 'The new comparative economics', *Journal of Comparative Economics* 31, 595–619.

Dooley, M., D. Folkerts-Landau and P. Garber (2003) 'An essay on the revived Bretton Woods system', NBER Working Paper 9971.

European Central Bank (ECB) (2001), *Monthly Bulletin*, May.

Frankel, J.A. (1999) 'No single currency regime is right for all countries or at all times', NBER Working Paper 7338.

Freund, C. (2000) 'Current account adjustment in industrialized countries', Board of Governors of the Federal Reserve System, International Finance Discussion Paper 692.

Gács, J. (2000) *Macroeconomic Developments in Hungary and the Accession Process*, Interim Report, March; available at http://www.iiasa.ac.at/Publications/Documents/IR-00-013.pdf.

Goldstein, M. (2003) *China's Exchange Rate Regime* (Washington, DC: Institute of International Economics).

Halpern, L. and C. Wyplosz (eds) (1998) *Introduction in Hungary: Towards a Market Economy*, (Cambridge: Cambridge University Press); available at http://hei.unige.ch/wyplosz/intro6.pdf.

Ho, C. and R. McCauley (2003) 'Living with flexible exchange rates: issues and recent experience in inflation targeting in emerging countries', BIS Working Paper 130.

Hölscher, J. and J. Stephan (1999) 'Exchange rate policy, fiscal authority and integration prospects: the Hungarian case', in H. Gabrisch and R. Pohl (eds), *EU-Enlargement and its Macroeconomic Effects on Eastern Europe* (Basingstoke: Macmillan), 151–73.

Joint Statement of Russian–US. Economists (2000) *New Agenda for Economic Reform in Russia. Transition* (Washington, DC: World Bank/The William Davidson Institute/Stockholm Institute for Transition Economie), May–July.

Kaser, M., (2006) 'East Germany's economic transition in comparative perspective', in J. Hölscher (ed.), *Germany's Economic Performance: From Unification to Euroisation* (Basingstroke: Palgrave 1994)

Kornai, J. (1997) 'Adjustment without recession: a case study of Hungarian stabilization,' in S. Zecchini (ed.), *Lessons from the Economic Transition: Central and Eastern Europe in the 1990s* (Dordrecht, Boston and London: Kluwer), 123–53.

Krugman, P. (1988a) 'Pricing to market when the exchange rate changes', in S. Arndt and J.D. Richardson (eds), *Real-Financial Linkage Among Open Economies* (Cambridge, MA: MIT Press).

Krugman, P. (1988b) *Exchange Rate Instability*, Lionel Robbins Memorial Lectures (Cambridge, MA: MIT Press).

Krugman, P. (1991) 'Target zones and exchange rate dynamics', *Quarterly Journal of Economics* 106(3) pp. 669–82.

Kulkarni, K. (1999), 'Determination of the Chinese yuan rate: an analysis of foreign exchange transactions', *Indian Economic Journal* 48(3).

Obstfeld, M. and K. Rogoff (1995) 'The mirage of fixed exchange rates', *Journal of Economic Perspectives* 9(4), 73–96.

Olson, M. (1993) 'From communism to market democracy: why is economic performance even worse after communism is abandoned?', in H. Siebert (ed.), *Overcoming the Transformation Crisis* (Tübingen: J.C.B. Mohr), 3–31.

People's Bank of China (PBoC) (2003) *China Monetary Policy Report.*

Rajan, Raghuram G., and Arvind Subramaniam (2005). 'What undermines aid's impact on growth?' *Working Paper*, National Bureau of Economic Research (NBER), No. 11657, Cambridge, MA.

Sinn, G. and H. -W. Sinn (1994) *Jumpstart: The Economic Unification of Germany* (Cambridge, MA: MIT Press).

Sommer, A. (2005) 'China's currency under valuation', in J. Hölscher and H. Tomann (eds), *Globalization of Capital Markets and Monetary Policy* (London: Palgrave).

Svensson, L.E.O. (1992) 'An interpretation of recent research on exchange rate target zones', *Journal of Economic Perspectives* 6(4), 119–44.

Tikhomirov, V. (1997) 'Capital flight from Post-Soviet Russia', *Europe–Asia Studies*, 49(4), 591–615.

Walsh, C. (2003) 'Implications of a changing economic structure for the strategy of monetary policy', Speech held at a symposium on 'Monetary Policy and Uncertainty: Adapting to a Changing Structure', Jackson Hole, Wyoming, Federal Reserve Bank of Kansas City.

Williamson, J. (1994) *Estimating Equilibrium Exchange Rates* (Washington, DC: Institute for International Economics).

Williamson, J. (2003), *The Renminbi Exchange Rate and the Global Monetary System* (Washington, DC: Institute for International Economics).

Xie, A. (2003) *Global Economic Forum* (New York: Morgan Stanley).

Index